Alive for Sure

A JOURNEY OF REDEMPTION!

By: Suzanna Warren

ISBN: 9781726736077
Imprint: Independently published

Unless otherwise noted, Scripture quotations are taken from the following:

Printed in the United States of America

Cover design by GreenStreet Marketing Battle Creek, Michigan

Contents

Acknowledgments

My gratitude first and foremost goes to my Heavenly Father. He is the one who set me aside in my mother's womb and never took His eyes off me...despite all the times I turned my back on Him and told Him I wanted nothing to do with Him.

I then thank every woman and man God ever put in my path to help guide me to where I stand today. I know I have not been easy to love or direct. A very special thanks to all the people who answered the call, to challenge and encourage me to be all the woman I am today.

Because I was such a tremendous mess, God had to send a lot of His Angels to pull me back from the gates of hell. If you happen to be one of them, I thank you from the bottom of my heart.

I know I also hurt a lot of people along my many roads to destruction. If you are one of them, please forgive me. Had I been in my right state of mind, I would have never done the things I did. Hopefully, my redeemed life is proof that I am truly sorry for any pain I caused along the way.

I dedicate this to all those who are still suffering from anything that is stealing their peace and distracting them from God. Although you may feel like you are alone, you are not. Many other women are experiencing the same thing you are, and if you are willing to reach out, I will gladly take your hand and help you become all you were meant to be.

May you be radically blessed, healed and made whole as a result of sharing your life in the following pages. This journey is not just mine, but yours as well.

When they call on me, I will answer;
I will be with them in trouble.
I will rescue and honor them.
Psalm 91:15 NLT

Introduction

And He said to her, "Daughter, your faith has healed you
Go in peace. Your suffering is over!"
Mark 5:34 NLT

This workbook is not about glorifying all the poor choices I made over the years; it is the redemptive story of how loving and caring our dear Heavenly Father is.

The pages that follow are a detailed account of the last 51 years of my life. They can be graphic at times so please do not leave it laying around for young eyes to read. Being an abused woman without a conscience for many years caused me to do some things I would never have done in my right state of mind.

I would like to say I never maliciously set out to hurt anyone however that was not always the case. Unfortunately hurting people hurt people and one thing became very clear as I wrote this material, I did things that hurt people along my journey. Because I didn't know how to care for myself and get out of bad situations properly, I stayed in unhealthy relationships and brought about a lot of pain to some innocent people including my own daughter.

As much as I would like to be able to go back and change the way I did things, I cannot. But what I can do is take my experience, strength, and hope and share it with you. I can walk with you and help you address every demon that has tried to destroy you. I cannot do it for you, but I can help you fight. I can encourage you to keep going when you want to quit. I can support you when you are scared and listen when you want to talk. I can also love you when all you want to do is cry.

As you can see from my story, it does not matter what you have done; God is the great Redeemer. He does not love me more than you. He loves us both the same.

The question now becomes are you ready to see what He can do with all of your choices. I promise you, just as He recreated my life into its amazing state, He will do the same for yours. He specializes in messes like us. Are you ready and willing?

The Year of the LORD'S Favor

Initial Self-Assessment

Isaiah 61:1-4

The Spirit of the Sovereign LORD is upon me

What would it look like to have the Spirit of the Sovereign LORD be upon you?

____

____

____

Because the LORD has anointed me

What would it look like to be anointed and would you want that?

____

____

____

To proclaim good news to the poor.

In what ways do you feel poor?

____

____

____

He has sent me to bind up the brokenhearted,

What has broken your heart?

____

____

____

To proclaim freedom for the captives

In what ways do you feel like a captive?

____

____

____

And release from darkness for the prisoners.

What is your darkness? What makes you feel like a prisoner?

____

____

____

To proclaim the year of the LORD's favor

What would the LORD'S favor look like in your life?

And the day of vengeance of our God

Where do you want to see God's vengeance?

To comfort all who mourn

Where do you need to be comforted?

And provide for those who grieve in Zion

What is causing you to grieve?

To bestow on them a crown of beauty

How would your life be different if you had a crown of beauty?

Instead of ashes

What ashes do you need to surrender to Jesus?

The oil of joy

What would your life look like with the 'oil of joy'?

Instead of mourning,

What is causing you to mourn?

And a garment of praise

What would your life look like if you wrapped it in praise?

Instead of a spirit of despair.

What has caused you to have a spirit of despair?

They will be called oaks of righteousness,

What would your life look like being an oak of righteousness?

A planting of the LORD for the display of His splendor.

Imagine being planted by the LORD to be a display of His splendor.

They will rebuild the ancient ruins
What ruins need to be rebuilt in your life?

____

____

____

And restore the places long devastated;
What has been long devastated in your life?

____

____

____

They will renew the ruined cities
What would your ruined city look like if it was renewed?

____

____

____

That have been devastated for generations.
What in your life has been devastated for generations?

____

____

____

From Riches to Rags

I knew you before I formed you in your mother's womb. Jer. 1:5a

I was adopted into a middle-class family when I was just a baby. Before it was over, I had five brothers. I was my daddy's little Princess. I loved hanging out with him. As far as I was concerned, he was my knight in shining armor. My life seemed perfect.

My dad and older brothers drank all the time, so I thought nothing of drinking out of my dad's beer cans. I loved the way it tasted so I did it as often as I could.

As time went on, my mom and dad didn't get along. I always heard her yelling at him. Little did I know at the time, my dad was having an affair with a woman from work. All I heard while I laid in bed was my mother yelling at him while he never said a word. He finally left when I was 10. I knew it was my mother's fault. To make matters worse, my grandfather started violating my innocence at the same time.

I had no idea what to do with all the raging emotions I had within me. I did not know what else to do so I turned to the family liquor cabinet. I also started smoking both cigarettes and marijuana in hopes of alleviating some of the pain. The next thing I knew I was regularly getting kicked out of school for violating the policies. I was lost in the midst of my devastation and had no idea how to ask for help.

I would sometimes get to see my dad on the weekends. He hung out at the bars a lot, so I had a blast being with him. I met some misfit boys from the community and started hanging out with them. We would take my dad's alcohol and drink it. Life seemed wonderful when I was there because I could get intoxicated and he didn't care.

From that point forward, my life totally spiraled out of control. Not knowing what I was doing, I made a pact with the devil at 14 years old. I ended up in trouble with the law a short time later, was put in jail at 15, and then placed in foster care.

While I was there, I continued to make poor choices. I ended up participating in a lot of sexual encounters just because I thought it was the thing to do. The foster care home was an incredibly dysfunctional place. I finally had enough of how unfair it was so I contacted the State and asked them to remove me.

After a year and a half of being away, my mother allowed me to return home. I had a new respect for her and was willing to follow her rules. I was only there for the summer because she allowed me to run off to Texas with the young man I had met in foster care.

What was your childhood like?

If it was painful, how did you cope?

Who were the people in your life you went to for help?

Looking back, did they point you in a positive or negative direction?

If you didn't have someone to talk to, what did you do?

It's your turn:

Off to Texas we go...

My boyfriend was a nice young man. He had a heart of gold, but as is often the case, he too had his issues. His mother had left their family for another woman, and his dad liked to work and drink a lot.

He had a job offer in Texas so at the age of 17 and 18, we loaded up everything that meant anything and headed south. I was home free. We moved to a little shack out in the middle of nowhere. We were 45 miles west of Conroe in a little town called Plantersville.

There were several little shacks and trailers on the small piece of property where we lived. This gave me an opportunity to get to know the other tenants. I was a fun loving gal who was always up for a good time. It didn't take long for me to meet some other fun loving people who also liked to drink and have a good time.

Before I left for Texas, I asked my mother to give me the insurance card so I could get birth control pills. She was adamant that she wasn't going to make the State pay for me to play house. I thought I would fix her. When I ran out of my pills, I didn't try to find any more. The next thing I knew I was pregnant. That was the last thing my boyfriend and I wanted so we decided the best thing we could do was have an abortion.

Did you make bad choices as a teenager? ______________________________

What did you do about them?

____

____

____

Do those decisions still haunt you today? ______________________________

Would you be willing to talk about them? ______________________________

Do you think God can forgive you and heal all the pain associated with it? ______________

Right about the same time this happened, my boyfriend and I made friends with three brothers and two wives. They would put him to work out of town for a week at a time and then come to visit me on the side. I was friends with the wives and unfortunately didn't think anything of intermingling with their husbands. They acted as if they cared so much for me and my mate yet they were sneaking over for visits while he was out of town.

When my boyfriend returned home for the week, all I wanted to do was party. He only wanted to spend time alone with me. Being the good boyfriend he was, he would go with me and act like he was enjoying himself. When he drank, his unresolved issues from his past would trouble him and it drove me nuts.

It was at one of the weekend parties I met a good-looking stranger who really took an interest in me. Bad went to worse when I married him within a month of meeting him. He took me on a Tuesday to get married because my friends had every intention of stopping the Justice of the Peace wedding he planned on having the following Friday. I didn't know God at that point, but I had the worst feeling in the pit of my stomach...as if God was trying to stop me from making the worst mistake of my life.

I know the plans I have for you, says the LORD, They are plans for good and not for disaster, to give you a future and a hope.
Jeremiah 29:11 NLT

Not knowing what the feeling was, I married him. Why wouldn't I? Before getting married, we drank all the time, partied naked and lived like there was no tomorrow. We had such a good time hanging out together, how could this not be a good thing?

Immediately after getting married, I realized I had been taken hostage. There was no more partying naked, and I was not allowed to see my friends. I was told I had to get a job. A job? What was I going to do with a job? I sat in his apartment in College Station, Texas, realizing I had married a stranger. I had no idea who this man was; he obviously wasn't the same one I thought I knew before saying my vows.

What is the worst mistake you feel like you ever made?

____

____

____

What did you do when you realized you had made this mistake?

____

____

____

How do you think this decision altered the course of your life?

____

____

____

How do you think it has impacted who you are today?

Did you have people to help you walk through it? If so, who?

When you think about that part of your life, do you have shame and guilt you need to address? If so, are you willing to address it so you can be free?

It is your turn:

From Happily Ever After to Homelessness

I will instruct you and teach you in the way you should go;
I will counsel you with my loving eye on you. Psalm 32:8 NIV

Little did I know, the man I married was a massive alcoholic and drug addict. He was acting very strange one day. He wanted me out of the apartment, so he sent me to the store. In my clueless state, I did as he asked. When I returned too quickly, I caught him in the bathroom with a needle in his arm. Like a fool, I said, "If it's good enough for you, it's good enough for me," and stuck my arm out to him. That was the beginning of a 9-year nightmare. Before it was over, I ended up addicted to alcohol and marijuana, acid, cocaine and meth.

What have you done or tried in an attempt to be close to someone you cared for?

____

____

____

What happened to you as a result?

____

____

____

Looking back now, would you make those same decisions? ____________________

What have been the long term consequences of those decisions?

____

____

____

Being the controlling man that he was, he told me I had to give him all my paychecks. Little did I know, he used all the money to support his drug and alcohol habit. He was a man who used me for his gain, and I wasn't smart enough to know better.

I had a hard time keeping jobs. I was so insecure and had no confidence in myself. I applied for one job and was told to go to another apartment in the same complex in which I lived. I went over there, and my potential boss offered me some Crown Royal. The next thing I knew, there was another older married man on top of me. It was not at all a pleasant experience. I asked him what his wife would think of that. Needless to say, I wasn't invited back and I didn't tell my husband about it.

Have there been times when you found yourself in compromising situations? If so? How did you handle them?

____

____

____

How did you feel about yourself after the fact?

____

____

____

Did you try to take corrective action? If so, what did you do?

____

____

____

Battle Creek, here we come!

My husband was charged with three drunken driving offenses in 6 months, so we had to move to Michigan to escape his going to prison. I had to quickly learn to drive so I could get us out of there. He took me out after we had been drinking to teach me how to drive in the busy city of College Station. How I didn't cause a severe accident was obviously the grace of God watching over me. It took three times to pass my driver's test before they felt I was qualified to function behind the wheel. Once I received my license, we set out for his hometown of Battle Creek, Michigan.

Before we left Texas, I had stolen a foil picture of a set of praying hands. I didn't know God, but I knew those hands would keep me safe. Because I had such an incredible faith in those hands, I always tried to keep them in the car with me.

What have you used to keep yourself safe?

____

____

____

Do you believe God was with you through all of your escapades? ____________________

List examples of ways God has protected you:

____

____

____

Did you know it was God taking care of you or did you call it fate? Why?

____

____

____

I will lead the blind by ways they have not known,
Along unfamiliar paths I will guide them;
I will turn the darkness into light before them
And make the rough places smooth.
These are the things I will do; I will not forsake them.
Isaiah 42:16 NIV

It's your turn:

Pregnant?

My husband told me he couldn't have children so I stopped taking birth control. Within about a month, I was pregnant. This was the last thing I wanted. My only aspiration in life was to get drunk and pretend the nightmare I was living wasn't real.

Have you found yourself pregnant not knowing what to do about it? ____________________

What decision did you make? ____

How do you feel about the decision?

____

____

____

The entire course of our marriage was riddled with domestic violence. While I was pregnant, he threatened to kill the baby and then vomited on me while telling me how much he hated me. Somehow the baby and I survived the pregnancy.

We lived several miles from town, and he would disable the car so I couldn't drive. I would figure it out how to fix it and leave for the day. He would come home early and catch me being gone and then beat me and rip the phone out of the wall so I couldn't call for help.

Another time he punched me between the eyes while I was driving 55 miles per hour. When I stopped the car and got out, he left me on the side of the road 180 miles from home. Another time, he had a loaded gun pointed at my face, then turned to shoot the duck off the top of the television blowing a hole in our door.

He was also very abusive sexually. He would beat me up and then want to have sex. He never thought about my needs; it was only what he could do to please himself. The abuse was nonstop.

The madness continued until I had finally had enough. I took our daughter and left one night after he beat me and passed out. When he realized what happened, he took her from the daycare the following day. During that time, I proceeded to party like crazy. I met drug dealers who gave me piles of cocaine. After six weeks of this, my mother told me if I would get my daughter back, she would send me back to Texas to be with my friends. I convinced him to let me have her for the day, and I quickly flew back to Texas.

What have you tolerated while in relationships with others?

____

____

____

If you were mistreated, did you stay or did you leave? ______________________________

If you stayed, why do you think you did that?

____

____

____

What did you hope to gain from staying?

____

____

____

If you left, where did you go?

____

____

____

Did you go back after you left? If so, how many times? ______________________________

When I arrived back in Texas, my friends had become addicted to meth. Unfortunately, it wasn't long before I too was addicted. We drank and did meth nonstop. I couldn't care for my child and had no desire to do so.

She turned one-year-old while we were there and I had no idea it was supposed to be a huge celebratory event. Thankfully my best friend took care of that for me. She gave her a little cake and a small baby doll.

My ex finally sent people looking for me in hopes of retrieving his missing daughter. My life was a blur from all the drugs and alcohol. Because of the onset of meth addiction and my friend's suspicion that I was sleeping with her husband, she wanted my daughter and me out of their lives.

Thankfully I had a job at a gas station so I took her to work with me. Some Mormons came in and offered to take her home until I got out of work. They had me spend the night with them and then paid for a bus ticket to get us back to Michigan.

For He will deliver the needy who cry out,
the afflicted who have no one to help.
Psalm 72:12 NIV

I stayed with my mother for a week and made my way back to Battle Creek. I eventually ended up back with my husband. He assured me if I ever left with his daughter again, he would have me killed. Because he was so psychotic, I believed him and never tried to take her again.

As my life continued to unravel, he decided to divorce me and get custody of our daughter. When we went to court, I had a big bag of cocaine in my pocket and a loaded syringe in the car. I stood in the lobby thinking about going to court. I knew I couldn't be a mom to this child so I went back to the car, stuck the needle in my arm and drove back to the dope house where I was residing.

It's your turn:

I don't know where I am going....

He feels pity for the weak and needy,
And He will rescue them.
He will redeem them from oppression and violence,
For their lives are precious to him.
Psalm 72:13-14 NLT

My life was in shambles. I had a fierce drug habit I could not escape, and I bounced around to different drug houses. I decided the best thing I could do for myself was leave town. I planned to run away to Chicago to see what it had to offer.

In the process of trying to get out of Battle Creek, I had jumped in front of a car in the middle of the night desperate to get a ride. The man took me about a half mile from I 94 and told me he wasn't going any further. The next thing I knew; I was surrounded by police. I ended up spending the night in jail for opening and drinking a beer in front of the police officers.

The following morning, I called my ex-husband to get me from jail. I spent the day with my daughter and then tried to get him the drugs he wanted. When I was unsuccessful, he dropped me off at the entrance ramp of I 94. As I exited the car, my little girl was in the back screaming because she didn't want her mommy to go again.

I had to leave because I had nothing to offer anyone. I had no idea who I was other than a massive drug addict who had absolutely no idea how to be free. Desperate to find a new life, I walked down the ramp singing, "I don't know where I am going but I sure know where I have been...." by Whitesnake.

Do you have children? ____

How do you think your addiction impacted them?

____

____

____

A nice man in the military picked me up, took me north of Chicago and rented me a room. He told me the best thing I could do was to go home to my family. I told him I didn't have a family. I got a good night of rest and woke up the next morning ready to conquer the world. I called a nasty drug buddy from Battle Creek to tell him what I had done. He told me to get to a Western Union, and he would wire me the money to get home. He tried to scare me into not going to Chicago.

Another nice man picked me up trying to get to the Western Union. He took me grocery shopping with him and told me he would take me home; however he didn't think his wife would like that. He took me to the Western Union and gave me some tips as to what streets were safe and what streets were not.

I went into the Western Union to call my friend. He wasn't able to wire me the money so he told me to hitchhike back home. I went out and tried to catch a ride back to I 94. The man who picked me up told me he didn't know how to get there. I asked where he was going and he told me the beach! I had a new bathing suit so I went with him to the lake. I then proceeded to live with him for the next few months. He was a Cook County Sheriff.

What have you done to try to fix your problems?

____

____

____

How did it work out for you?

____

____

____

Because stability wasn't something I had known, I got bored staying with the sheriff in Chicago. I hitchhiked back to the drug house in Battle Creek for a week before returning to Chicago. I didn't bother to tell my new friend I would be away for a while. The next time I did it, he was done with me.

From that point, I started going to truck stops and hitchhiking wherever the drivers would take me. I have been up and down the east coast and along the southern coast from Florida to California. I had a blast seeing the countryside. That is until I was in a severe semi accident. We were going 100 mph when we hit a cow in the middle of the night. The next thing I knew; I was lying in a bed of fertilizer getting my leg cut free by the Jaws of Life. We were taken to the hospital. I lost a lot of skin on my backside. They poured something on my back to clean my wounds; it burned like crazy, but they wouldn't give me pain medication because of the needle tracks I had up and down my arms.

At that point, the people I was with gave me $100 and shipped me back to Michigan on my tummy in different semi-trucks. Once I arrived, my ex agreed to let me stay with him and my daughter while I healed. When it was time for me to leave again, the two of them begged me to stay.

Because both of us were raging alcoholics and drug addicts, we did not know how to function as a healthy couple. We continued to beat the daylights out of each other, lie and cheat on each other. Thanks to my new found independence I acquired while hitchhiking the countryside, I realized I did not have to tolerate his abuse. I found a job and left him permanently.

It's your turn:

Which one is God?

You must not make for yourself an idol of any kind...
You must not bow down to them or worship them,
For I, the Lord your God, am a jealous God...
Exodus 20:4-5a NLT

When I finally left my ex-husband for good, I was mentally and emotionally brainwashed and bent for destruction. I was 23 when I met a bar owner 27 years my senior. I had a blast chasing him and felt important being with him. I was finally somebody. He took me on a lot of trips. I was sold hook, line, and sinker.

He didn't like my drug habit and was afraid he would lose his bar because of it. I tried desperately to control my habit but just couldn't. I never knew when the obsession would hit. I was smart enough not to use drugs when I was sober but since I drank nearly every day, I was constantly a disaster waiting to happen.

When he caught me doing drugs, he would end the relationship and I would have to figure out what I was going to do to survive. It was during one of those times I met the man who became my sugar daddy. He drove a big town car and had lots of money and he didn't mind shelling it out for my drug and alcohol habit. Little did I know, the more money he spent on me, the more I became addicted to him.

It was while I was drinking at my boyfriend's bar that I met the gal who changed the course of my destiny by taking me to church. I didn't know what I was doing when I gave my life to Christ but I knew something happened to me as a result. I felt like I was high for two weeks. A high like I had never had before...it was amazing.

My significant other could have cared less about my new found life but when my sugar daddy found out about it, he came with a big pile of cocaine. I did it and lost that feeling I found in Jesus. I wanted it back so bad, I tried getting baptized, but that didn't work. I tried talking to the people at the church but they didn't understand. The only thing they could say was 'You are a new creation in Christ, the old is gone and the new has come.' Really? I know it came but it also went and I wanted it back. The problem was no one knew how to get me back to the feeling I had experienced as a new believer.

My new life was very tumultuous. The battle for my soul was in full effect. I drank a few beers and felt like I shot the president. When I went to church, I was told I was going to hell for everything I did. I had no idea how to live my new life; I just knew I couldn't stand all the condemnation I was experiencing. I finally left the church and went back to my old way of living.

Have you ever given your life to God? ______________________________

How did it happen?

____

____

____

What was the experience like for you?

____

____

____

Do you still feel connected to Him today? ______________________________

How would you explain your experience?

____

____

____

The Lord our God is merciful and forgiving,
even though we have rebelled against Him.
Daniel 9:9 NIV

My bar-owner boyfriend was controlling as well...only in a much different way! He didn't want me having my own friends or jobs. He said when I had money I got in trouble. Unfortunately, I wasn't smart enough to realize that I had again become a hostage of sorts.

He tried desperately to control my drinking in hopes of controlling any drug use that might occur as a result. The problem was, I had a raging monster that took over once I started drinking. Unlike other people who can have a few and go home, when I had a few, I wanted 12 more.

Cocaine addiction was another terrible thing that could occur once I started drinking. For whatever reason, at the worse possible times, I would start to believe the lie that I could do just a little bit of cocaine and be alright. The problem was, I could never do just a little bit, once I started, I was not stopping until the money was gone and I had no way of getting more.

This addiction caused division between my boyfriend and I. He would tell me he was done and my life would spiral out of control. Sometimes I had to have sex with drug dealers because I ran out of money. Because I was not raised that way, it felt a filth I could not wash off of me.

Do you think you have problems with alcohol and/or drugs? ______________________________

Do you notice it is hard to stop drinking/using once you start? ____________________________

Have you ever done anything you have regretted once you started using? __________________

Give an example:

____

____

____

It's your turn:

The darkness before the dawn

Those who trust in their own insight are foolish,
But anyone who walks in wisdom is safe.
Proverbs 28:26 NLT

In hopes of being somebody someday, I went to Beauty School. I wanted to travel the nation doing hair on stage. This is when I really started dressing provocatively and discovered I was cuter than I had been told. Not only did I realize I was cute, I also started using the brain I never knew I had. We had a great teacher who played games to engage our learning. Not knowing it at the time, I was very competitive. I had a blast competing with the smartest girl in our class for the top position. She would always get me by just one question. Imagine how I felt when we both went to State Boards and I passed, and she had to go back to retake them. I was absolutely elated that I had finally won!

While I was in beauty school, my boyfriend and I were on again / off again because of my drug habit. It was during this time that I picked up a guy from my self-help meetings and started having sex with him. I had judged one of the other beauty school students for getting pregnant again. It was shortly after that I found myself pregnant again! Because of my sick attachment to my 'bar owner boyfriend' and what he might think, I felt I couldn't keep the child so I dumped the guy and had my sugar daddy pay for an abortion. I then swept it under the rug and pretended it never happened.

Beauty School gave me an opportunity to make friends. Somewhat healthy friends at that! We became like a little family. The further I progressed in the program, the closer we drew to one another. It was incredible to feel like I finally belonged somewhere. I engrossed myself in my work and tried to be the best hairdresser possible.

What are some things you believe about yourself?

____

____

____

How do you think these things impacted your life?

____

____

____

Do you still think they impact you today? ______________________

If so, would you like to address them and find the real truth? ______________

In an attempt to control my shenanigans, my boyfriend made me a bet that I couldn't quit drinking until I completed beauty school. This was a 5-month bet. I went to a beauty show and lived it up right after I made the bet. I didn't consider this a violation because I lived true to it after the fact. I wanted my car, ring and trip he promised if I was successful.

For the next five months, I was sober and straight. Because he owned a bar, I was around alcohol all the time. I could not wait to drink again. His friends would taunt me about not being able to drink. I assured them the day would come and I too would be drinking again.

On graduation morning before the event took place, I had already started drinking Baileys and coffee. I was half trashed before the ceremony started. Once graduation was over, my new friends and I took off in the limousine my sugar daddy rented for me. He also provided all the alcohol I would need along with flowers and money.

My bar-owner boyfriend wanted no part of my special day. He was scared because his friends warned him not to let me start drinking again. They knew I would be out of control. As promised, I took advantage of my special day and got absolutely trashed. So much so, I evidently told him exactly what I really thought of him. I have no recollection of that taking place.

Have you had periods of sobriety? ____

What caused them to end?

____

____

____

Did you have secret people in your life you kept around for convenience sakes?

____

How do you feel knowing you have secrets?

____

____

____

Once I started drinking again, it only took about seven months before my life totally spiraled out of control. I drank every day and often ended up doing a lot of drugs. A few days after Christmas, my daughter busted the bathroom door open and found me with a needle in my arm and blood pouring everywhere. She screamed at me stating she knew I could not quit drinking.

What major experience caused you to want to seek help?

____

____

____

What steps did you take to improve your situation?

____

____

____

When I am in distress, I call to you,
because you answer me.
Psalm 87:7 NIV

It's your turn:

No longer a loser!

Get all the advice and instruction you can,
So you will be wise the rest of your life.
Proverbs 19:20 NLT

Eight days later, I was on an airplane headed for Texas so I could enter treatment. I spent 28 days there. I gave the program everything I had. I did not want to return to Battle Creek being the same loser I was when I left.

Every morning, I went to class to learn about the Big Book of Alcoholics Anonymous. I listened closely and applied what I learned. Before I left, I had worked the first eight steps which had included a 7-hour 5th step (5.5 hours of it about sex but I was convinced I didn't have a problem in that area). I could not figure out how I could blame the whole world for my problems and still get better...but it worked. In fact, it worked so well; I made student of the week before I left.

Give all your cares and worries to God,
for He cares about you.
1 Peter 5:7 NLT

When I returned to Battle Creek, I was a new woman. I went to my 12 step meetings every day...sometimes more than once a day. I made friends and they became like family to me.

Have you participated in self-help groups? ______________________________

Which groups have you attended?

____

____

____

How do you feel about them?

____

____

____

Do you think they have helped you? ______________________________

I stayed in contact with the male counselor I had done my step work within Texas. He saw me through many of my difficulties in early recovery. In fact, to me, he was Jesus with skin. I felt safe with him because I had done my 5th step with him. I thought he was good looking and told him I would like to lay him out and 'do him' in front of the whole class. I'm sure that statement didn't help our situation. The only thing that saved us from going to bed together was the 1100 miles between us.

This counselor was many things to me. He directed me in many areas of my life. Because sex was a big problem for me, he always tried to keep me on the right course. With him helping me make all my decisions, I didn't have to learn how to make my own.

Who are the people in your life helping you make decisions?

____

____

____

How did you meet them?

____

____

____

How healthy are they for your recovery?

____

____

____

Do they let you figure out problems for yourself or do they do it for you?

____

____

____

As I made my way through early recovery, I started asking questions about my male counselor. He didn't want me having sex, yet it was alright for him to do it. When I questioned him about it, he told me it was my religiosity. My what? Neither of us was married so I couldn't figure out why it was alright for him to engage sexually and not me. He was Catholic and I was Protestant but that shouldn't have mattered...as far as I knew, we both served the same God just in different churches. Because I couldn't make peace with some of his bizarre ideas, I started to separate myself from him.

This was an interesting transition because he had become a god to me. One of the last times I picked up a stranger, I was lying in his bed after being highly disappointed by his performance dreading the thought of telling my male counselor I had failed again.

Here I was, a woman proclaiming to follow God and yet I am not the least bit concerned about Him being upset with my behavior. It is no wonder God felt the need to show me it was time for the counselor to be removed from my life.

Who in your life is like a god to you?

____

____

____

How do you think God feels about your affections for this person?

____

____

____

You must worship no other gods, for the LORD,
whose very name is Jealous,
is a God who is jealous about his relationship with you
Exodus 34:14 NLT

It's your turn:

Time for a change

Do not be unequally yoked with unbelievers.
For what partnership has righteousness with lawlessness?
Or what fellowship has light with dark?
2 Cor. 6:14 ESV

As I continued to grow closer to God and work my recovery program, I knew I needed to make some changes in my life. I could tell God was prodding me to end my relationship with my bar owner boyfriend. I was scared to death to do this because he had money. He didn't share it with me but would come through if I was in an absolute crisis. I found myself giving God 75% of my life and him the other 25%. I had no idea how to let go of the man and totally trust God.

One day while I was at my 12 Step Meeting, there was a flyer for a 6-week sex course at a local church. I knew this was an area I struggled with and wanted desperately to hear what God had to say about the topic.

When I arrived at the 'well to do' church, I was wearing an itty bitty black spandex mini skirt with my high heels, my hair was bleach blonde, and my fingernails were long and nicely manicured. I pranced my way right to the front of the church so I could pay close attention to all God had to teach me.

It was at that church that I learned Christmas was Jesus' birthday and I started to learn how much He loved us. It was totally unlike the other church that brought such heavy condemnation against me.

Before I knew it, I met this wonderful woman who wanted to teach me all about Jesus. My appearance didn't stop her from wanting to pour the love of God into me. It seemed her only mission was to teach me about Jesus, the love of her life.

He sent out his word and healed them,
and delivered them from their destruction.
Psalms 107:20 ESV

Who has poured the love of God into you?

____

____

____

How did it feel?

____

____

____

Did they accept you for who you were or did they try to change you? Explain:

____

____

____

As God continued to work in my heart, I heard a sermon about Peter walking on the water. The pastor challenged us to get out of the boat to see if we would sink. It was then I knew I had to end my relationship with my bar owner boyfriend. I had to 'try God' and see if He could really help me live on my own. I returned home and broke up with him a short time later.

Even though I felt like we didn't have anything in common anymore, it was still a hard transition for me. I had to go through a grieving process.

Trust in the Lord with all of your heart
And do not depend on your own understanding.
Seek His will in all you do
And He will show you which path to take.
Proverb 3:5-6 NLT

Are you close enough to God that you would know if He was asking you to give up someone or something that was causing you harm? ________________________________

If you are, what is God asking you to give up so you can be free?

____

____

____

Are you willing to let go of whatever it is? ________________________________

Why do you think He would be asking for it?

____

____

____

Could it be He cares about you and sees it is harming you? ______________________

How do you feel when you think about the last question?

____

____

____

As I look back on this season of my life, I wanted to be close to God but I didn't have a clue how to make that happen. I went to church all the time and tried desperately to live what I was learning; unfortunately, I was so full of bad programming, I never knew how I was going to behave. Thankfully our God is a very gracious God and He sees what we are going to become...and loves us immensely every step of the way.

It's your turn:

I am going to be your WHAT?

Beware of false prophets,
who come to you in sheep's clothing
but inwardly are ravenous wolves.
Matthew 7:15 ESV

Unfortunately, it was only a short time later that my man problems went from bad to worse. On my way to the bar to dance one night, I asked God to help me meet a really cool guy. Sure enough, I met him ... and practically moved him in that night. Little did I know at the time, it wasn't God who answered that prayer!

Have there been times when you just got free from one bad experience and then found yourself in bondage to another? ____

Give an example:

____

____

____

I longed to be with my new boyfriend because he would pray with me and cry. He had a soft touch and dropped perfume off in my mailbox. He wasn't afraid to buy me gifts as an expression of his love...and I so longed to experience the feeling of love.

Because I had so many unhealed areas in my life, I would have sex with strangers as a means of coping with my out of control emotions. Because I knew this wasn't something I should be doing, I would go home and journal about it. My boyfriend would stay at my house while I worked and read everything I wrote (emotional rape). He would then use it against me when he was upset.

While I was with him, he bought me three diamond wedding rings. I was madly in love with him. I wanted to have his baby and live happily ever after like all the other pretty families at the church. I knew that we too could be a happy family like all of them. God was not so convinced. He kept telling me to watch out for the wolf in sheep's clothing. I didn't know what He meant. How could he be a bad person? He prayed with me and made me feel so loved...when he was there.

In the midst of trying to figure out what I wanted, I somehow managed to get involved with my bar-owner boyfriend again, so I spent countless hours trying to figure out which man was best. Do I pick the one who has all the money but never shares it with me or do I pick the good lover who buys me gifts? I would take my days off and cry because I couldn't figure out which one would be best for me. I even went so far as to go to a fortune teller to help.

I finally picked the one who bought me diamond rings. Because I still needed tons of healing, I sent my other boyfriend a letter breaking up with him. I had informed him that I had met a nice Christian man and planned to marry him. Little did I know, God had other plans!

After receiving my 3rd diamond ring, I decided to ask God to give me clear cut specific directions as to what to do. Within 24 hours, I was being choked in my bathroom while hearing him tell me I was going to be his f***ing wife. I told him I wasn't going to be his f***ing anything and he needed to get out of my house NOW!!! All this happened while my little girl who I had on the weekends was coloring Easter eggs on the other side of the wall.

Needless to say, my decision was clear. It kept me rattled for a while but then loneliness took over again. Every now and again, I felt like I needed a boyfriend fix. I would call him and we would have sex. The problem was I would feel like I had a huge black hole within me after he left.

Looking back, can you recall times when God tried to warn you about the relationships in your life? ____

What did you do with His warning?

____

____

____

What happened as a result?

____

____

____

Once he was out of my life for good, I went into deep depression. The good thing that eventually came from it was I pretty much stopped using sex as a means to comfort myself. It took a long time before I was 100% but I made progress. The closer I grew to God; the more painful sexual experiences would be. It got so bad before it finally ended that I would cry if I engaged.

I had to learn that I didn't have to have sex with people just because they wanted it. What I didn't know about myself at the time was that I really just wanted to be loved. I was so psychologically and spiritually maladjusted that I didn't know I was going about it in all the wrong ways.

What do you do to try to alleviate your pain?

____

____

____

Have you found that your coping strategies work for you? ________________________________

Can you see yourself being totally free from the things that hold you back? _______________

How would your life be different?

____
____
____

It's your turn:

School of hard knocks

For I do not understand my own actions.
For I do not do what I want, but I do the very thing I hate...
...For I have the desire to do what is right
but I don't have the ability to carry it out.
Romans 7: 15, 18b

Because I wanted to be someone important someday, I went back to school to get my G.E.D. Being the determined person I was at the time; I quickly accomplished that goal so I could start college the following fall.

The night before my GED graduation, I was rollerblading in downtown Battle Creek minding my own business, or so I thought. I met this great looking stranger with beautiful teeth. The next thing I know; he is in my apartment having sex with me. Because I knew I wasn't supposed to do that, I felt horribly guilty after the fact. I was so mad at myself for failing again; I allowed these feelings to take all the joy out of my graduation the following day.

Have you made mistakes that knocked you off course? ________________________________

How did you handle them?

____

____

____

How long did you allow your mistake to impact you? ________________________________

How did you correct the problem?

____

____

____

The following fall, I started college. I wanted to be a counselor but had bad motives because of all the abuse I had suffered. I wanted to counsel men so I could mess them up like I felt they had done to me. Thankfully as I continued to grow closer to God, I became aware of what He wanted me to do with my life and it was NOT to counsel men!

I also continued to build the relationship with the well-to-do family who helped me from the church. Not only did they take me in as one of their very own, but they also helped clothe me in more appropriate attire and they loved me with God's love. Despite the fact I was so different from them, they didn't act like they were afraid of me. They spent holidays with me and taught me what healthy families were supposed to look like. It was at their house one Christmas when God told me I would get to be an evangelist.

I was so excited that God had chosen me that I was ready to leave immediately for Moody Bible College. Here I still smoked and swore like a sailor but I was ready to do whatever necessary for my God! I was willing to leave everything if that is what it meant to be in my Daddy's will.

"My thoughts are nothing like your thoughts," declares the Lord.
"And my ways are far beyond anything you could imagine."
Isaiah 55:8 NLT

Have there been times when you felt God was directing you to something bigger than you? Explain the situation:

____

____

____

How did you handle it?

____

____

____

Not really knowing how to let God into my life to change me, I locked myself up in my apartment and read self-help books. I would then go to my 12 step meetings and really think I was someone special. After all, I was now an Evangelist!

Someone gave me a Christian book to read challenging God. I was to ask Him for three things and then give Him a year to answer the prayer. I picked the three biggest things in my life: I wanted a husband, a driver's license and my child returned to my care. As the year came to a close, I was livid with God for not giving me what I had demanded.

Don't let this throw you.
You trust God, don't you?
John 14:1 Message

What steps have you taken to fix yourself?

____

____

____

Have you tried to control God? ______________________________________

What was the outcome?

____

____

____

How do you think it impacted your relationship with Him?

____

____

____

It's your turn:

Relapse

When pride comes, then comes disgrace,
But with humility comes wisdom.
Proverbs 11:2

Pride had gotten the best of me so I quit going to my 12 step groups. As far as I was concerned, they were nothing but a bunch of sinners and I didn't want any part of them. I went faithfully to church and tried to live up to everything the preacher taught. Little did I know, I was a toxic bomb because I had so much unresolved anger and pride. I had no idea how angry I was at God because He refused to give in to my demands.

Then came my day to fast for the new church. I had really bad PMS and an infected tooth. I called a friend for a script for antibiotics and Vicodin. Drinking my juice and taking my Vicodin, I set out with good intentions. That was until my friend backed out on our scheduled shopping trip. I furiously wandered across the street to Kmart. I had just received my student loan check and wanted to spend it. I bought a bunch of junk I didn't need and then met a good looking stranger, who happened to be a stripper in the checkout line.

He wanted to carry my stuff to the car so I had to explain I didn't drive. One thing led to another and I proceeded to relapse! I decided that I should leave town. As I was leaving, I heard an audible voice asking if I was afraid of what might happen. Thinking it was an odd question at the time, I proceeded toward a neighboring town so that no one would know what I was about to do. God was not about to let me hide in another town and misbehave; He saw fit to make sure people I knew saw me.

Because I walked out from underneath God's umbrella of protection, I re-activated the mental obsession of my addiction and could not quit thinking about drinking. Four days later, I relapsed again. At 7:00 am the following morning, I went to the grocery store to get another six pack of beer and a pack of cigarettes. Sure enough, there was a member from my 12 step group walking in as I was walking out. He asked how I was doing...which I thought was a stupid question! How did it look like I was doing?

Just a week ago, I thought I was a good Christian girl. In the course of 5 days, I met a stranger, drank, started smoking cigarettes again, smoked $750 worth of crack, drove drunk without a license to the crack house, pawned all my jewelry and bent over for the drug dealer for a $20 rock. I also missed all the other social obligations I had as a result of rebuilding my life the last two years. I felt like a disgraceful, shamed-filled mess without hope!

For all that is secret will eventually be brought into the open,
And everything that is concealed with be brought
To light and made know to all.
Luke 8:17

What mistakes have you made that led you to believe you were without hope?

___

___

___

What did you do to try to pull yourself back together?

___

___

___

How well did it work for you?

___

___

___

Call to me and I will answer you and tell you great
and unsearchable things you do not know.
Jeremiah 33:3

A few hours later, I called my ex bar owner boyfriend to help me. I explained I had totally unraveled over the last few days and needed to get out of town. As we were going down the highway, an audible voice asked me who I was trying to run away from because I could not run away from myself. I totally freaked out and told him that I had to go to a self-help meeting.

I found one in a town close to where we were traveling. There was this obnoxious guy at the meeting I could not stand. When he shared, he talked about shame. I then realized I was so full of shame; I could not stand myself.

Give an example of your trying to run away from your problems.

___

___

___

How well did it work for you?

How has God intervened in your life when you were off course?

What did you do as a result?

What shame are you still carrying?

It's your turn:

Request # 1: Starting Over - My child comes home!

...Forget all that-It is nothing compared to what I am going to do.
For I am about to do something new.
See, I have already begun!
Do you not see it?
Isaiah 43:18-19A NLT

I returned to Battle Creek and started over; however, I failed to get rid of the stripper I met a month earlier, I had two hits off a joint. It was at that point I kicked him out once and for all. My previous relapse took away all my pride. The last thing I wanted to do was relive that nightmare. Thankfully that was on May 4, 1996. I have not had a drink or used drugs since that date.

When was the last time you had a drink or drug?

____

What was the result of your using?

____

____

____

Do people know about your use? ______________________________

Do you find that you have to hide it? ___________________________

Do you feel like you are done with it for good or do you have reservations?

____

____

____

Hope deferred makes the heart sick,
But a dream fulfilled is a tree of life.
Proverbs 13:12 NLT

Two weeks later, God brought my daughter back to live with me. Life was very difficult because I did not have a driver's license. I really struggled to get both of us everywhere we needed to be. Because I still didn't know how to ask God for help, I went to my ex. He told me if I didn't spend the night with him, he wouldn't take my girl to school for me. I was furious and went to my self-help meeting to cry and whine about how difficult my life was to manage. Thankfully God showed up and had one of the other members take my girl back and forth for the last six weeks of the school year.

I then lost my job because I would not have sex with my boss. I was so mad at God because I had to go on welfare. I would have wrung God's neck if I could have gotten my hands on Him and I wasn't afraid to tell Him so. I didn't understand at the time that God was providing me an opportunity to get to know my little girl better. I was so obsessed with what He wasn't doing; I couldn't see what He was doing.

Was there a time when you were asked to jeopardize your integrity for a favor?

____

____

____

How did you handle it?

____

____

____

How did you feel after the fact?

____

____

____

God was gracious about bringing my daughter home, but I didn't have the first clue how to care for her needs. I was a terrible mom. I yelled all the time and was so stressed out about what God wasn't doing for us that I didn't know how to appreciate the things He was doing. Everything was so difficult; I truly hated my life. I couldn't drive so I constantly had to ask for rides. We didn't have a washer or dryer so we had to have people take us to the laundry mat. I didn't have daycare so I had to figure that out every day. I was so desperate; I would send her with people I had never met before so that I could go to work. I truly believed life sucked and I hated it. It was so hard. I had such a victim mentality, and I never thought I was going to escape being poor and miserable.

God and I fought so badly during this season of my life. I truly felt like I hated God and was forced to have a relationship with Him. If I tried to walk away, I knew I wouldn't be able to stay sober so I had to put up with what I perceived to be His abusive ways of dealing with me. I continued to trudge on despite how much I hated my life.

After the relapse, my counselor from treatment suggested I take a month break from church because I had become too religious. When I started going again, I tried a new church. Not long after I started attending, they asked if I would be interested in starting a substance abuse group.

I ordered a step book that totally changed my life. When I did the material to prepare for my class, I realized how mad I was at God for the way He was running my life.

One day while I was ranting and raving about how poorly He treated me, I heard an audible voice ask, "When are you going to see everything you are going through is to prepare you for the people you will be working with in the future?" Wow! That shut me up and made me think about things a bit differently.

Have there been times when you were really mad at God for the way He was running your life?

____

If so, how did you handle your upset?

____

____

____

It's your turn:

A new role to play

My dear sisters, be strong and immovable.
Always work enthusiastically for the Lord,
for you know that nothing you do for the Lord is ever useless.
1 Cor. 15:58 NLT

I started the 12 step group at the church and was on fire for God. I truly wanted to help women get better. For whatever reason, the church assigned me a co-leader. She was older than I was and unfortunately, we did not click at all. What I wanted to be a wonderful experience turned out to be somewhat of a nightmare as far as I was concerned. I allowed her strong personality to control me and affect the way I led the group. It felt like my self-esteem was taking constant hits.

Once the first group was started, we started a co-ed 12 step Christian sharing meeting modeled after the other 12 step meetings. I really wanted to start this group because some people complained about my sharing Jesus in the other meetings.

Despite the continual healing Jesus was doing in my life, I was often still an emotional mess. When I started to go off the rails, everyone knew about it. I would sit in meetings and share exactly how I felt about things sometimes at a very high octave. I had a very filthy mouth and it offended some of the women in the meetings. My co-leader tried to talk to me about it but I had no idea how to change and frankly didn't like being told what to do.

Although the group only lasted a season, I allowed her to impact the way I lived for several years. The inside of me would crawl whenever I had to be around her. We would make attempts to resolve our problems but I never felt like we ever reached a resolution.

One day I prayed and asked God to show me what the problem was. I saw a vision of her standing in the doorway blocking it. I was outside of the room and all the ladies were in the class. Instead of going back to God for more insight as to what to do with that vision, I allowed her to take over and I stepped back.

Have you found yourself in situations with people who were controlling? ___________________

How did you handle yourself?

____

____

____

How did you respond when they tried to correct you about a defect?

____

____

____

Name instances where you allowed stronger personalities to control you:

____

____

____

How did you feel about yourself after the fact?

____

____

____

After my upset with the church group, I started re-engaging with the other 12 step group again. I started doing women's groups with the book we used at the church. The groups became like little families. I could be very honest about my life because I wanted the other women to be honest about theirs as well.

We decided we would be called the God Squad. We were 'fishers of broken women.' The problem was when I finished one group, I would start another and the ladies from the first group eventually dispersed and went back to their old ways of doing things. I didn't know how to properly care for them long term.

Have you ever been in a small group? ________________________________

What was it like for you?

____

____

____

Were you able to connect with the other people in the group or did you feel like an outsider? Explain:

____

____

____

How do you feel about this group?

____

____

____

...Let us not neglect our meeting together as some people do,
but encourage one another,
especially now that the day of His return is drawing near.
Hebrews 10:25 NLT

It's your turn:

Request # 2: My Driver's License

The LORD says, "I will give you back what you lost...
Joel 2:25a

After I had been sober again for a year and a half, I decided it was time to try for a restricted license. The people at my 12 step meeting kept telling me I would never get it back on the first try. I told them I worked for the King of the Universe so we would see about that. I went home and got on my face to pray. I told God I would be really upset if He didn't give me my license back the following day. I had been following His rules and not driving. I had honestly been trying to do life His way. I couldn't bear going any longer without being able to drive.

Thankfully God came through for me. I had seven very influential people in the waiting room of the Secretary of State willing to walk in and testify to my new way of life. God knew I was serious about my recovery because I had been involved in starting the substance abuse groups at the church and I was honest about my use when questioned. It was the best birthday present God could have ever given me. Even better, a State rehabilitation service bought me a van and paid for six months of insurance and license plates. I felt so special and loved.

Talk about a time when you really wanted God to do something for you:

____

____

____

Did He do it for you? ____

How did you respond to the way He answered your prayers?

____

____

____

After I received my restricted license, I felt so special. I wanted more than anything to obey God. Part of my driving restrictions included taking the most direct routes to and from my assigned destinations. I had a membership to the gym around the corner from my job. Unfortunately, it was not on my way home. I pondered the idea of taking that way home ... until I heard, "What will you tell the officer when you get in an accident going around the corner?" Needless to say, I never drove myself to the gym.

How do you respond when you believe God is instructing you to do something?

____

____

____

What do you think would have happened if I would have disregarded what I thought God said to me?

____

____

____

Living every day ordinary life...

She rises while it is yet night and provides food for her household...

Proverbs 31: 15a

During this time, I went to work every day and took care of my daughter at night. The data entry job I had was mentally challenging. Because of my past experience with waitressing, bartending and hairdressing, I was not used to using my brain this way. I had to go to my van at lunch to rest because my brain felt like an overloaded sponge that couldn't take another drop of liquid. My head ached from trying so hard to learn my responsibilities.

One of the things that was difficult about this job was a few of the other women who worked there. They were very mean to me. I am not sure what the problem was but it was hard to endure. Because I had such a happy go lucky personality, I went to work early every morning and went through the facility greeting everyone and wishing them a happy day.

As time went on, I got somewhat better at my job. I tried my best but because it was so fast paced and overwhelming, I made some mistakes. Unfortunately, my gem of a boss had to correct my mistakes which made her job all the more difficult. Even though this job was hard for me, I showed up every morning and tried my best.

Over time the mean gals started to soften. I worked desperately to pour the love of God in their direction. After I worked there for several months, some of us lost our jobs due to corporate cutbacks. It was somewhat sad but also a relief. One of the mean girls that I had come to care for also lost her job. I knew I worked for God so I would be alright, but she had been there for years and was really devastated. I attempted to instill hope, and I stayed in contact with her for a while.

If you are working, what do you think of your current job?

If you don't like it, what else would you like to do?

What would be your dream job? Why?

What would it take to get you there?

What do you do when you can't stand the people you work with?

It's your turn:

My 12 Step Chum

God wants you to live a pure life. Keep yourselves from sexual promiscuity. Learn to appreciate and give dignity to your body, not abusing it, as is common among those who know nothing of God
1 Thess. 4:3-5 The Message

Despite the fact I continued to grow close to God, I was still desperate for a husband. I was so sick of having to make all of my own decisions; I just wanted someone to come along and make my life better. I also wanted to engage sexually with someone. Not realizing how stupid my request was, I would beg God, "I will take anybody, just give me somebody."

It would aggravate me to hear someone say, "You are such a good looking gal, I don't know why you are single." Talk about making me mad. I was single because God wouldn't let me have a man!!! Truth be told, I wasn't ready for one but you could not have convinced me of that.

As I continued to attend my meetings, I became fond of one of the other members. We liked to play mind games with each other. He would hang out with me when he was separated from his other girlfriend. I didn't have sex with him because I knew God didn't want me to do that anymore. I was waiting for marriage.

One night, a bunch of people from the 12 step group were going out dancing. I took my daughter to an all-night babysitter. On the way to meet my 'friend' for our first legitimate date, I visualized myself grabbing the front of God and ripping Him off His throne. I told Him I had this and would see Him in the morning.

I proceeded on my date. I was more provocative than I had ever been. I was dancing like I actually knew how. My friend was sure this was going to be the big one. We left the crowd behind and took off for another bar so we could dance alone. On the way, we were starting to slip off the edge with our behavior.

It was at the second bar that God jumped back on His throne and intervened. As the words, 'Lick it so we can kick it' played in the background, I heard "So you're really going to go do this, you are going to walk out of here and do that and face all the people you are going to have to tell." It freaked me out so I told my date we had to repent. He was not a happy man but I was ecstatic that God saved me from making a terrible mistake. I was so pleased with myself because I didn't go out of the bar and finish what I started in the car, I called the evening a success. He, on the other hand, called it sex and called me a liar!

Because my behavior was so out of control that evening, I felt like God wanted me to make amends to some of the people from my 12 step group. I went back to them and did so. One gal had hoped I was able to get what I was after. When she found out I didn't, she had choice words for me.

Talk about a time when God tried to save you from making a terrible mistake:

____

____

____

At the time, did you know it was God trying to intervene in your life? ______________

Did you heed His warning or did you ignore it? ______________________

What happened as a result?

____

____

____

Did you have relationships that were impacted? Explain:

____

____

____

God used this experience to get me on the right track, but it didn't help my desire for a mate. I had absolutely no idea how to be happy being single. I truly believed my life wouldn't be so difficult if I had someone to share it with.

To prepare me for what was ahead, God had me move in with a friend from church. She had offered previously but I was not interested. I had wanted to buy a trailer in a park but felt like that wasn't the right thing to do. The night before the deadline for registering my daughter in a school, I heard an audible voice tell me I was going to my friends. I was now all for it because I felt like God chose that to be our next place to live.

It was a beautiful house out by a country club. I felt like 'somebody' getting to live there. My friend had a very good job as an engineer. I really liked her and was happy that God used her during the next leg of my journey. She had another roommate that wasn't real fond of me or my yelling. This caused some upset in the household but I didn't much care.

When I got mad at God, I wasn't afraid to tell Him. I had set up an area in the basement for my workout machine. I would get on my stepper and scream at God. Looking back, it is a wonder He didn't allow the floor to collapse. I certainly would have deserved it.

While I was at my friends, I continued to immerse myself in the church, my 12 step groups and my friends in recovery. Unfortunately, I wasn't real close to my daughter because I didn't know how to be…and being a good mother was not an aspiration I had at the time. Thankfully, she drew close to the roommate that didn't like me and they became pals.

Discuss a time when you felt God led you to a course of action:

____

____

____

What happened as a result?

____

____

____

It's your turn:

One last detour!

Ask me and I will tell you remarkable secrets
you do not know about things to come.
Jeremiah 33:3 NLT

One day, as I was leaving the sanctuary at church, a gal asked if I was single. I told her I was and wondered why she asked. She knew someone she wanted to set me up with so she requested my number.

I walked away all excited but then started thinking about my friend from the 12 step meeting. What if he wanted me? I needed to give him a chance to have me. I called the gal back and told her not to give him my number.

For the next three months, I started hanging around with my friend from the meetings again. Before it was over, I had an engagement ring on my finger and a wedding dress hanging in my closet. I was getting ready to go to Florida for Spring Break and wasn't about to blow things with God again. We would be getting married before we took any trips!

The strange part of the story is that we were polar opposites and not in a good way. I was totally out of debt, he was not and it didn't bother him. I worked full time, he was on disability. I was very active and he was not. I would ask him to take me hiking and he always promised he would, just not that day. I tried to eat healthy and he liked greasy foods. The only thing we both liked was playing mind games with each other...and that didn't benefit either of us.

As I read my new book "Be Anxious for Nothing" by Joyce Meyer, I started thinking about what I was doing. I would be out running and feel like I couldn't get oxygen. I started thinking that if I married him, I wouldn't be able to flirt with anyone ever again. I talked to his sister in law to see what she had to say. She asked if I respected him. As I pondered the question, I realized I did not. I then went to my female recovery friend's house early one Sunday morning and told her I had to get the ring off my finger because I couldn't do it.

I gave the ring back but asked him not to return it to the store in case I changed my mind and wanted it back again. I continued to pray and made an appointment with the prayer pastor at our church. I asked God to use her to tell me exactly what He wanted me to do. It didn't take long at all. She told me, "Get away from him, stay away from him, don't call him and don't talk to him." As my eyes widened from her firm direction, I agreed to do what she said.

I returned home and got on my face to pray. I told God I was truly sorry for wanting so desperately to marry my friend. I understood I had made a terrible mistake and agreed to be back on His potter's wheel for another couple years. For the first time ever, I was happy with my singleness.

Have you ever been single for a period of time? ______________________________

If so, what was it like?

____
____
____

If not, why?

____
____
____

What do you think about being alone?

____
____
____

If you don't like it, why do you think that is?

____
____
____

Have you ever been in relationships and still felt very alone? ____________________

Why do you think you felt that way?

____
____
____

If you are currently in a relationship, write about it:

____
____
____

Do you believe your mate is one God would have chosen for you? ________________

If not, would you be willing to end the relationship if you knew for sure God didn't want the two of you together? ______________________________

Don't look out only for your own interests,
But take an interest in others too.
Philippians 2:4 NLT

If your current mate isn't the one, do you believe God could provide the perfect mate for you? Explain your answer:

____

____

____

Do you realize you are causing harm to both of you by staying in a relationship that is not divinely inspired? ____

What do you think about the last question?

____

____

____

It's your turn:

Request # 3 - The Long Awaited Marriage!

Then the LORD God said, "It is not good for the man to be alone. I will make a helper who is just right for him."
Genesis 2:18 NLT

The very next day, that same gal from the church who wanted to introduce me to someone before followed me out of the sanctuary. She asked me what I was doing that day and informed me the man she wanted me to meet would be at the 2nd service. She wanted to know if I would be interested in meeting him. I was excited.

When I laid eyes on him, I about melted. He was very attractive to me. He was younger than my 12 step friend and looked like an adventurer. We made arrangements to go on a date that evening. We went and saw Heaven's Gates and Hell's Flames. I couldn't tell you anything about the program. All I remember is how happy I was getting to be with this guy.

We saw each other three more times over the course of the next ten days before I left for Florida on Spring Break. By that time, I was pretty sure he was the man God had chosen for me. Looking back, I wonder if the reason I knew so soon was because I tended to flirt with strangers when I traveled. Knowing my chosen man was back in Michigan waiting for me, I didn't want to do anything to violate my long awaited treasure.

We continued to see each other. Three months later we were engaged and two months after that, married. Premarital counseling was one of our wedding presents. Unfortunately, I was so prideful at the time I didn't pay attention to what was being taught. I knew there would be nothing that could happen to us that God and I couldn't work through together!

We both initially agreed we would do it God's way and wait until we were married to engage sexually. After we said our vows in the company of many witnesses and celebrated for a short time, we took off to the cabin where we would consummate our marriage. I was pretty nervous to say the least. It had been a long time since I had sex...and those other times didn't matter like this would. After all, this is the man I had chosen to be with for the rest of my life. My husband thought it was great to see how timid I was that first time. Timid or scared stiff?

Our honeymoon gave us an opportunity to get to know each other. I wanted to have sex all the time because it had been so long since I engaged. This drove my new husband crazy. He tried to accommodate me but you could tell he thought enough was enough.

My husband had a house that wasn't ready to live in yet. It was way out in the country on 14 acres. We spent a lot of time working on the outside of the property when we should have been working on the inside. This caused some tension to say the least.

Thankfully my previous landlord was willing to allow us to live with her while we continued to work on the house. All went well until she had a leak that was in major need of repair. It was at that point that my new brother-in-law allowed us to live in a trailer he had bought. I was not a fan of our new housing arrangements. I had lived in town by the country club, and now I had to drive several miles every time I went anywhere.

My husband shared his affections for me with his job. He worked long hours which really upset me! Unfortunately, my fairy tale wasn't everything I had dreamed it would be. I was very rigid about dinner time. He would work late, and I would have supper waiting for him. I would be furious when he finally arrived. One day he had the audacity to inform me his other girlfriends had always been so happy to see him when he finally arrived. Really? I wanted to throw plates at him and cause great bodily damage...because that is what I felt he was doing to me every time he was late. It got so bad; I would get myself worked up before it even happened and then be a mess for the next several hours.

What was wrong with me? I thought for sure that my life was now going to be all better because I had the man I had awaited all those years. I just knew he was going to be my new savior and make me the happy woman I longed so desperately to be.

Because I didn't know how to be content on my own, I expected him to jump through my many hoops to keep me happy. After all, I believed it was his job now that I was his wife. The problem was, I had no idea what would make me happy so how could I expect him to know. Unfortunately, we lived like this for a long time because I had no idea how to change.

Just a few years before this, I couldn't be happy because I didn't have my three things I had demanded from God: The child, the license and the husband. Now I had all three and I was still miserable.

Have you had times when you were convinced if you only had certain things, you could be happy? Explain:

____

____

____

Did they make you happy?

____

____

____

Looking at your life right now, would you say you were happy? ________________________

What do you think it would take for you to be happy?

____

____

____

Do you understand happiness is an inside job? ______________________________________

What would you say is currently standing between you and happiness?

____

____

____

I stood in church singing songs about God being all I needed while assuring Him there was no way I could live without my husband. Without realizing what had happened, I made my husband my new god.

It's your turn:

The Stabilizer in Action!

Fathers, do not provoke your children to anger by the way you treat them.
Rather, bring them up with the discipline
and instruction that comes from the Lord.
Ephesians 6:4 NLT

My daughter and I continued to have a venomous relationship. I would scream and holler trying to get her to obey. My husband came from a stable family and didn't condone our toxicity. He was a mild mannered individual but he was firm. He refused to let a 13-year-old or his new bride control him.

Parenting was another area where life was difficult. My daughter gave him a run for his money. She had two drug addicted, totally unstable parents prior to his arrival so she had no idea what to do with stability.

I had issues at my job so I finally quit. Instead of getting another job, we decided I needed to stay home with our daughter to steer her in the right direction. While I was home with her, I started going back to school to complete my education. This gave me something meaningful to do and gave my husband a break.

When our daughter was 15, her behavior was out of hand so we finally had to put her in Teen Challenge. She was only there for a couple of months before getting kicked out of their program. Once that happened, she went to live with her dad for a month. When she came back home again, she knew we meant business. She started following our rules and life began to smooth out tremendously.

Do you have children? ____

What do you think of being a parent?

____

____

____

Do you have stepchildren? ____

Do you allow your husband/boyfriend an opportunity to parent your kids? __________

Explain why or why not:

____

____

____

I continued to engross myself in my studies and my husband worked all the time. The tension between us grew. I would say that he had his world, I had mine and we had ours together. However, when he wanted to take a trip with his buddies, I would have a fit about the cost. The thought of letting go of large sums of money so he could enjoy himself would bring the worst out of me...but he never said a word when I spent hundreds of dollars going to see Joyce Meyers or Beth Moore.

It seemed the farther I went in school, the more distance there was between us. Our daughter was old enough to do her own thing so we didn't have to worry about her. I had lots of friends so I was pretty lost in my own world much of the time as was my husband lost in his. This went on for quite some time.

In my delusional state of mind, I thought I had the perfect marriage. In fact, I had my husband up on a pedestal. Then came the day I found out about his porn habit. I was devastated. The news came days before I left for a Christian Counselor's Conference with three other women. I was so ashamed of what I had discovered; I didn't want to talk about it with anyone.

When I went to the conference, I bought numerous books about the topic. I did it secretly because I didn't want to talk about what had happened. I did my best to pretend all was well.

When I returned from the trip, my husband and I took off on a work trip to Colorado. I was still pretty heartbroken over the whole ordeal so I couldn't be myself, whoever that was. I felt like I needed to be guarded and protected from further hurt. I tried to be cordial but it was most difficult.

When we returned from the trip, I was laying out in the sun reading the books I had bought at the conference. More than anything, I wanted to be healed from this nightmare. As I tried desperately to process the material, I felt God wanted me to give Him my broken heart. I did what He told me and He healed the situation.

Within a few months, I found out I was pregnant. My daughter called my husband at a party and told him I had taken a pregnancy test. I didn't think anything of it because I had been having sex for seven years without protection. Why would I be pregnant now? Sure enough, I was and we were all floored. My husband was furious I took the test without him. I tried to explain I was sure I wasn't pregnant.

Again our marriage changed. After the baby arrived, we worked opposing shifts so we didn't see much of each other. I was very lonely. This went on for a few years until we determined we had to do something different. Thankfully my in-laws went out of their way to take care of our daughter so we could have some time alone.

At one point I was so fed up with our bickering back and forth, I threatened counseling. He thought it was a great idea. I called the counselor from the church. When we first arrived, the counselor told us he prayed and felt God wanted us to work on love. LOVE! As sad as it was to admit, I realized I didn't know how to love my husband. When he was gone a lot, I learned how to do life without him so we merely co-existed. That revelation was a huge turning point in our marriage.

Another thing that helped was my continued desire to get well. When I realized there was something wrong with me, I wanted to go after it to get it resolved. As I continued to become an emotionally healthier woman, my husband started falling deeper in love with me. He jokes that it only took 14 years for that to happen.

My husband was chosen by God to love me and walk with me through many years of painful territory. Because I had been hurt by so many men, I did not know how to let him near my heart. I could sometimes let him in but sometimes I was as cold as ice toward him. He continued to love me despite the way I treated him. It was hard for many years because he didn't know what to expect when he got home. Sadly, it took about 18 years before I would start eating without him.

It's your turn:

God's Chosen Position: Drug Court

I will instruct you and teach you in the way you should go;
I will counsel you with my loving eye on you.
Psalms 32:8 NIV

I continued and finished my Bachelor's degree. I wanted to do in-home work like I did during my internship. I applied for a couple of positions but did not get them. I went to one interview that ended early due to my felony conviction. I was totally defeated at that point because my friend who wanted me to work with him assured me he had told the management about my criminal record.

A short time later, a gal at a recovery meeting told me I should get a job at Drug Court. I told her there was no way I wanted to work there. I had been in so much trouble with the law and had been before almost every judge in the court house. If God wanted me to work at Drug Court, He would have to put me there because I was not going on my own...

A few months later, I was at a brainstorming session for community recovery when I met the Drug Court coordinator. She told me she would try to help me get a job at the Substance Abuse Council. When that didn't work, I offered to help her at Drug Court until I could find another job. I told her about my criminal history; she did not think it would impact me. She pulled up my record in the system and it said 'dis' next to my felony charge. She then asked the court to run a background check to see if I could volunteer for her until I found a job.

Much to my surprise, my record came back clear. I volunteered for five months and was then hired part time so I qualified for the full time position when it became available the following fall. Before I was hired full time, I felt a strong need to write the Drug Court Judge a letter informing him of my criminal history and letting him know I would love to take the position should it be offered. When I filled out the application, I was instructed by my boss not to document the felony because it had been dismissed.

When I started volunteering there, I was very inexperienced. I believed almost everything the participants told me. I wanted desperately to help them get better and live productive lives. They would manipulate me and I wasn't any wiser until my boss got involved. I would then be furious because I had again been deceived.

After I worked there for a few years, I had my boss run my criminal history to see what was on it. To my amazement, it didn't have my 3 DUIs, my countless driving without a license or my reckless driving offenses but it did have the Attempted Uttering and Publishing felony we thought was dismissed. My boss went to administration for direction. They wanted to terminate my employment for lying on my application. There was an investigation and thankfully I was able to keep my job. Had I not written that letter to the judge years earlier admitting to my criminal history, I would not have been so fortunate.

While I was working at the Drug Court, I became very entangled with my boss. We both had our issues and for whatever reason, I felt an overwhelming need to help her fix what I saw as being wrong. We had similar personalities so at times the work environment became quite hostile. Things were not discussed in a healthy fashion so I was always trying to figure out what was real. When I wasn't at work, she would call for something and I would get emotionally distraught and stay that way for several hours.

Who in your life gets you rattled? ____

How do you respond?

____

____

____

Do you feel like you are entangled in someone else's life? __________________________

Do you want to break free from it? ____

If you don't want to break free, explain why you want to stay in the situation:

____

____

____

If you do, what have you done to try to break free from it?

____

____

____

What are you gaining from being in this relationship?

____

____

____

How would life be different if you walked away from it?

____

____

____

As I continued on my path to wellness, I started to see that I needed to separate myself from the unhealthy entanglement with her. It was not my job to fix anyone else. I didn't even have the ability to fix myself without the help of God and yet I wasted countless hours trying to fix her.

Thankfully God saw fit to do some rearranging and moved her to a new job and put a new boss in place. A male case manager whom I had previously worked with took her position. We had somewhat of a brother/sister relationship so it made the transition smooth. It was a much more relaxed environment after he took the reins. He believed I knew how to do my job and would only intervene if he saw things I was missing.

It's your turn:

Baby and a trip to the Wilderness?

Children are a gift from the LORD;
They are a reward from Him.
Psalms 127:3 NLT

While at Drug Court, I went back to school to get my Master's Degree. I did my internship at the church we attended. As my program drew to an end, I kept hearing that I was going to have another baby. This was the last thing I wanted because I was such a horrible mom and really felt like I hated most kids. They were loud, obnoxious and stole what little bit of peace I had. I told my groups I thought God wanted me to have a baby and felt sick about it. I would then celebrate every month when I started my period.

One month after I graduated, I became pregnant. I was so tired I had to take numerous naps throughout the day. I couldn't eat healthy food because the thought of it made me sick. There was a part that excited me but there was also a part of me that wanted my husband to raise what I thought was going to be our boy so that I could live happily ever after in my new career as a counselor.

As the months passed, I got more excited about the idea of being a mom. I was 40 years old and ten years sober. I had never been happier. I really felt like I had accomplished my dreams. I felt like I could now conquer anything. My oldest daughter had been accepted in the Coast Guard and was scheduled to leave about 12 weeks after the baby's arrival.

When the day finally came to deliver the baby, imagine the surprise on everyone's face when we discovered I had a girl. This was not at all what I had expected. I knew I was having a boy and he was going to do life with his Daddy. In shock I said, "A GIRL!"

Shortly after we had our little gal, our oldest left for the Coast Guard. My husband switched shifts so our little one didn't have to be in day care. God led us to leave our church and attend what used to be my husband's church in another town.

Shortly thereafter, I quit leading my small group because I 'thought' I was supposed to help start a recovery group at the new church. I didn't know at that time that it was not what I was called to do. It ended up being a disaster. I was overzealous because I knew how much the steps could change a person's life because they changed mine.

I tried to befriend one of the ladies in the group who admitted to having multiple personalities. She turned on me and it got very ugly. Because I was making a lot of my own decisions without the help of God, I got sucked into a terrible mess. Instead of walking away, I agreed to stay on and help until the program was launched for the public. It was an excruciating last few weeks because that is not what I was supposed to be doing.

What have you been asked to do that didn't have the outcome you had hoped it would have?

____

____

____

How did you handle the situation when you realized it wasn't going your way?

____

____

____

Do you think God knew it was going to turn out like it did? ______________________

Looking back, how do you think God was involved in your situation?

____

____

____

Here I was with a master's degree, a new baby, my oldest several states away, my husband on an opposite shift, and no support group because of my decision to help start a new group in a different city! Little did I know, God planned to use this new season to strip me of everything I had believed about myself.

Just a few months before this, I 'felt' like a strong, educated Christian women with many friends and a happy marriage. I would work out for a few hours at night and really enjoyed my new found life. Now I tried to help addicted people by day and had to learn how to love and care for a little girl I didn't know I wanted at night. My status as a popular gal at church was gone because I had a new role...and it wasn't anything I dreamed of having. I wanted to be spectacular. I wanted to be somebody who made a difference. I didn't want to be stuck at home feeling trapped raising a child.

My life as I knew it changed. I went to work and came home. For some time, I was miserable. I didn't understand at the time this needed to happen so God could recreate me into who He called me to be. God's plans for me that would never have materialized without my painful time in the wilderness.

When we left the church, I knew all the right things to say. By most outward appearances, I looked like a Christian woman who had everything in order. I was at the church often in small groups and I worked diligently to get my ladies praying for the needs of others. Do you think I dropped to my knees to pray? Of course not! I was too busy making calls, delegating that task to others. I knew God worked…I just didn't take the time to develop my own personal relationship with Him. I knew all the right things to say and do. I knew the rules to follow. Some may have even called me a Pharisee.

Has God ever called you to leave your comfort zone for something new?

____

How did you handle it?

____

____

____

It's your turn:

I'm the one who said I wanted to be close to God!

...I have loved you with an everlasting love;
I have drawn you with unfailing kindness
Jeremiah 31:3 NIV

All my female relationships disappeared due to my new role as a mother. Little did I know, God had to make room so He could work in my life. I was very lonely for a long time. In the process, I began to notice that God and I started to have a different sort of relationship. God wanted things from me that I didn't want to surrender. He asked me to give up coffee until we sold our house. I would get mad because I felt He was taking too long, so I would drink a cup of coffee and then have to confess.

God and I had this wild relationship. Over the next few years, He started wanting me to give up all my false gods. On that list were things I used to pacify myself from my supposed misery: Caffeine, chocolate, shopping, and the Visa card. The more He wanted, the more I felt stripped. I could be compliant for a season but then I would get upset about something and relapse usually with caffeine. I would then feel awful.

During this lengthy season, God showed me how much He truly loved me. He didn't beat me up for the things I did wrong. He desperately wanted me to come near to Him so He could love me to wholeness. He wanted to help me get to the bottom of why I felt the need to go to other things when I had Him readily available at all times.

Why did I think I needed those other gods to make me happy?

____

____

____

Why do you think God wasn't enough to satisfy my deepest longings and desires?

____

____

____

What do you turn to when life doesn't seem as satisfying as you want it to be?

____

____

____

As you have drawn closer to God, have you noticed 'it' doesn't satisfy you like it used to?

____

Why do you think that is?

____

____

____

Finally a Friend

Two are better off than one,
For they can help each other succeed.
If one falls, the other can reach out and help.
But someone who falls alone is in real trouble.
Ecclesiastes 4:9-10 NLT

During this long season of my life, I re-engaged with a friend I had met in my Master's Program. As time went on, we became major shopping buddies. Neither of us needed a single thing but that didn't stop us from hunting for treasures. I taught her about second hand shopping and all the wonderful bargains one can find. We acted as if it were a sport. I had so many clothes, I didn't have a place to put them but that didn't stop us from hunting for more.

Although I had a lot of fun with her, the time came when God started showing me we weren't healthy for one another. As God continued to refine me for what was next, I felt Him leading me to separate myself from the relationship. I knew I wanted all God had to offer so I was willing to do as He directed. I told her we needed to part ways. I don't think she was happy with my choice but I had to do what God wanted me to do.

Evaluate your relationships. Are they supportive of your new lifestyle? Explain:

____

____

____

Can you see how they have hindered choices you have wanted to make to be healthier?
Explain:

____

____

____

Have you felt God directing you to put an end to certain friendships because they aren't healthy? ____

Are you willing to lay them down for the sake of the new YOU?

Do not be misled:
"Bad company corrupts good character."
1 Corinthians 15:33 NIV

It's your turn:

It is time to finish what I started!

Trust in the LORD with all of your heart
And lean not on your own understanding;
In all your ways submit to Him
And He will make your paths straight.
Proverbs 3:5-6 NIV

Once I told my friend we needed to part ways, life again became very lonely. It was during this time God started prodding me to start the process to get licensed to be a counselor. I had been out of school for about seven years. I first had to get the felony off my record if I had any hope of being licensed.

Because God wanted this done, He allowed me to make contact with the prosecutor who was running for election. I talked to him and then felt led to write him a letter telling him my story. When he became elected, one of the first things he did was help me reduce my felony to a misdemeanor so I could be licensed.

I contacted a woman who supervised counselors and met with her a few times. She was very academic and we did not click. I met with her a final time over coffee. She told me I didn't need a license for the work I wanted to do.

I took what she said to heart and was willing to disregard the whole idea. That was until I started praying about what was discussed. It was a matter of seconds before God straightened me out regarding what 'He' wanted. It was during that prayer time I felt God directing me to a new supervisor for my licensing.

Talk about a time when you went to someone for help and they misguided you:

____

____

____

What happened as a result?

____

____

____

Once I met with the new supervisor, I started working on my hours. Over the next few years, I did what I had to do to complete the task I had been given. When I was about two-thirds through my supervision, I started studying for my test. I joined a study group with one of the therapists from the local mental health organization. I went to the group faithfully with a friend. We both scheduled our tests for the same day and our teacher drove us to the testing facility. My friend passed and I had to return to retake it.

As much as I had studied, the material did not make sense to me. I am a tactile learner and tried so hard to understand the material just by reading it. My teacher did not like to lose so she bought me new materials and met with me every Thursday afternoon. We processed cases to make the material come alive. The following December, my teacher took me back to retake the test and I passed! According to her, I tested two standard deviations above the mean! I say that smiling because it was some of the material I had to know for the exam and because it makes me sound really smart.

It was a relief to finally have the test behind me. I had studied every night for the previous six months and was tired of it. My little girl had also asked when I would be done so I could be with her again. Unfortunately, a lot of things had to be put to the side so I could accomplish what I felt I was instructed to do.

After the holidays, I applied for full licensure to be a counselor. It wasn't something I necessarily wanted for myself but did it because I felt like God asked me to do it for Him. Because of my criminal background, I had to write a letter explaining how I had made the necessary changes to become an upstanding citizen.

When my license came in the mail, I was totally blank on the inside. It was a polar opposite of what I was like when I received news I had passed my State Boards for Cosmetology. I could not understand why I was not happy about this accomplishment. I worked very hard and had absolutely no feelings of excitement. It was at this point that I realized something was not right about me.

What have you worked really hard for?

____

____

____

How did you feel when you finally reached your goal?

____

____

____

Did you cherish your accomplishments for a period of time or immediately find something new to do? Explain:

____

____

____

Do you currently have goals and aspirations? ______________________________

What are they?

____

____

____

If you don't, why?

____

____

____

Then you will call, and the LORD will answer;
You will cry for help, and He will say: Here am I.
Isaiah 58:9a NIV

It's your turn:

Why can't I feel?

He heals the brokenhearted
And bandages their wounds.
Psalms 147:3 NLT

I realized I had a problem. I did not know how to feel positive things. I had become emotionally calloused without knowing it. That would explain why people could have great things happen and I would feel blank emotionally. The sad thing is I did not just do it to them; I also did it to myself.

Without realizing what happened to me, I had again fallen into the groove of life. I did what I was supposed to do but was not really living the adventure. I was bored and miserable most of the time. In the midst of my existing, I did not realize I was simply going through the motions of life.

I did my studies every morning when I could stay awake for them. Looking back, I cannot tell you I was asking God to expose my upset. As Joyce Meyers would say, I was not who I wanted to be but thank God I was not who I used to be. I felt like I was stuck in the corridor headed to some unknown place that was never going to arrive.

As I continued to trudge on, I really wanted God to do something miraculous. I wanted to see clients and wanted to be of value to women. I did not want to merely exist. I desperately wanted God to do something with me so I could serve His people.

Ironically, I would ask Him how I was supposed to do ministry when I felt like I could not tolerate some people. I was so sick of sorting out lies and deceit at work that I closed myself off from feeling. I did my job and tolerated those whom I deemed hopeless...desperately awaiting the day I could walk away and serve God full time in greener pastures.

As I continued to beg, He started working with me in the area of LOVE. God wanted to teach me about His love so I could be of maximum usefulness to His people.

God had me get connected with a pastor in town that was all about loving the less fortunate. The pastor was a dear sweet lady that always told people how much she loved them and wanted the best for them. She saw some potential in me and asked if I would be interested in helping some of her ladies. One thing led to another and I was leading a group of super cool ladies through a process of dumping their baggage. The ladies were pretty faithful to the group and I was totally elated God was finally using my talents. The sweet pastor even asked me to speak at the Good Friday Service. She even gave me a financial gift for doing so. I was on top of the world.

In the midst of all the excitement, I again failed to seek God's direction for my future. I got lost in the pastor's promises to help me. Where I went wrong was clarifying what that help would look like. Because I failed to do that, I had expectations that didn't materialize. The end result was my being devastated.

Little did I know, all of this happened because God wanted to move my family in a new direction. He allowed the pastor to invest in me and teach me about God's love. He took what I perceived as a terrible thing and used it to move us into His will.

In July of 2017, God directed us to go to a new church (my old church where I was so involved) and leadership group. God directed me not to do ministry for the entire nine weeks of the training. As I sat through the class, I struggled with what 'I could do to get my ministry up and running!' On the 8th week, God had a gal from my group write a check for $1000 for the startup expenses.

Again, I should have been elated with excitement, but I wasn't. I was a little bit excited but nothing compared to what should have been. God then had others give money and gifts to the ministry as well...and again, I wanted to feel a lot of excitement but it just wasn't there like I thought it should have been.

It was during that time that God told me I didn't know how to let Him love me BIG. He was absolutely right. I didn't expect big things because I didn't want to be disappointed. I had lived a great deal of my life believing I wouldn't be anything more than I was right then so the hope of a great future full of marvelous blessings was little more than a fantasy.

God used the next year of my life to straighten out my distorted thinking and heal my damaged emotions. He has slowly but surely been teaching me it is a good thing to feel and experience emotions other than anger and rage. He has poured His love upon me in ways I could only imagine and drawn me so close to Him that I sometimes feel like I am illuminated with His Presence and Joy. Now more than ever, I want to go and help His women. I want to share His love with whoever He leads my way. He has clearly shown me that He has amazing things planned for my life if I will stay close to Him and follow His lead.

How healthy do you think you are emotionally?

____

____

____

Do you struggle with your emotions? __________________________________

If so, which ones?

____

Do you struggle with other people's emotions? ____________________________

How do you handle feeling uncomfortable?

____

____

____

Do you involve God in your emotions? ______________________________________

How do you feel about your current place in life?

____

____

____

Do you think God cares about where you are currently? ____________________________

Knowing what you know about God, what do you think He would change in your life?

____

____

____

For I know the plans I have for you, declares the LORD,
Plans to prosper you and not to harm you,
Plans to give you a hope and a future.
Jeremiah 29:11 NIV

It's your turn:

Food addiction?

...I am allowed to do anything but not everything is good for me
Even though I am allowed to do anything,
I must NOT become a slave to anything.
1 Corinthians 6:12 NLT

Food addiction is something I struggled with for years. It started in a desperate attempt to control my sexual nature. I decided it would be best if I started eating large amounts of food. I irrationally believed if I got rid of my sexy body perhaps that would help me behave better.

Mind you, I hadn't been sober that long so my body desperately craved sugars. I would buy large cans of peanuts and huge bags of M & M's and mix them together in a jar. In an attempt to soothe all my internal aches and pains, I ate, and I ate, and I ate some more.

When I worked at the Red Cross, they had a snack room. We were allowed to eat whatever we wanted from the room. My desk was full of wrapped goodies that I again used to soothe my upsets.

For the next couple decades, I used food as a comforter. Whenever I felt uncomfortable in any way, I ATE! I would be full but that wouldn't stop me from eating more.

Through this lengthy session of my life, I started to obsess about the way I looked. My tummy would get huge so I would try to control my eating. Only to again fail when I got bored or troubled. I worked out to counteract the results of all the food. I started getting cellulite on the front of my legs and I absolutely hated it but even that wasn't enough to get me to stop bingeing. I worked out so much I hurt myself and had to seek medical attention but that wasn't enough either.

There were times when I was willing just to give up because I didn't think there was any way I could lose the extra 10-20 lbs. I had gained. I believed I was doomed to have a big midriff because there wasn't any hope of being skinny again.

After 20 years of binge eating and exercising, I started reading about 'clean eating.' The author reported that exercise only does so much. Until we get our eating under control, we are fighting a lost cause. I started to consider what she had to say as I looked at what I thought was my huge stomach.

At the age of 51, I went to a new trainer and decided I was going to do something about the stomach I didn't like. He put me on a 1500 calorie daily eating plan and I almost went into shock. I ate that much for breakfast. He also asked me to drink a lot of water and only work out three times a week as instructed.

I could not believe my ears. 1500 calories! I knew for sure I would starve. I drank so much water that I constantly had to run back and forth to the bathroom. Because I couldn't believe three simple 20 minute workouts would help, I added some walking and a swim in on the side. The next thing I knew, I was absolutely starving and had to drink two gallons of water to suppress the hunger pangs. That is because I did not do as he instructed.

In the first week, I lost a belt loop around the waist. I was blown away by his methods. My problem was I still had a food addiction that wanted to rule my life. Although my body was starting to shape up nicely, the raging monster within would still rear its ugly head and sabotage my efforts.

After I resigned from my job of 15 years, I started really investigating why I could not control my appetites. A gal I met recommended the book 'A more excellent way' by Dr. Henry W. Wright. A couple of weeks after I resigned, I sat with my daughter and ate a scone. I felt very guilty for eating it because I knew there wasn't a thing about it that was nutritional. I started praying and felt like I was supposed to read the section on Addictive Personality. In that section, he talked about all addictions being rooted in lack of self-esteem, insecurity and the need to be loved. According to Dr. Wright, 'Excessive eating is a direct result of not feeling good about yourself.'

Do you struggle with food? ____

Do you use it as a comforter? ____

How do you feel after the fact?

____

____

____

Have you put on weight as a result of your eating? __________________________

How do you feel about yourself as a result?

____

____

____

Do you want to change your eating habits? _______________________________

What would you want to change?

____

____

____

Do you like to work out? ______________________________

What do you do now to stay in shape?

____

____

____

Would you be interested in joining a group for physical wellness? ________________

What would you like to do in the group: Run Walk Bike Weights Swim Cardio

It's your turn:

My obsession to be beautiful!

Don't be concerned about the outward beauty of
fancy hairstyles, expensive jewelry or beautiful clothes.
You should clothe yourselves instead with the beauty that comes from within,
The unfading beauty of a gentle and quiet spirit which is so precious to God.
I Peter 3:3-5 NLT

When I was a young girl, they didn't make clothes like they do today that fit me properly. Because I was tall and skinny, my pants were always too short, and my haircuts looked like a bowl had been placed on my head before the cut.

I looked at the other girls in my classes wishing I had boobs and hips like they did. Instead, I was just a homely stick figure who didn't really connect with anyone.

Once I started smoking pot and drinking, my concerns about being pretty stopped for a while. Sexual behaviors distracted me from caring about how I looked.

As I entered my late teens, I was often around older people. Because of my partying nature, I didn't care about food. I ate to survive so I didn't carry any extra weight. For whatever reason, I attracted people and they seemed to like being around me.

Once I met and married my ex-husband, life changed. I wasn't comfortable being me anymore. I allowed him to treat me in ways a loving husband would never think of treating his wife. After five years of abuse, I left him feeling like there was absolutely nothing pretty about me. I didn't have an ounce of self-esteem left. I read Cosmopolitan Magazine wanting to be pretty like them. I was willing to do what they did to be like them.

When I worked as a waitress one of the prettiest gals there acted like she hated me. I had to pray like crazy for her because she was so mean. My prayers really worked because we became best friends and lived together for a while. She taught me how to dress in a sexy fashion. I started getting my hair and nails done. I wore short skirts and high heels. I started to feel pretty...and I started attracting a lot of attention from men.

These new behaviors distracted me again. I started sleeping with who I wanted to sleep with and made a game out of it. My ex told me I was not any good in bed so I set out to learn...and what better to do that than practice!

It wasn't until years later that I realized all of my sexual activity wasn't the best thing for my self-esteem. Unfortunately, I lost my identity for a number of years. I associated sexy with pretty so as long as I felt sexy, I was all set.

For years I desperately wanted a boob job. I knew if I had boobs, I would really be pretty. The man who was willing to pay for them said I had to let him play with them. I knew for sure I would get in trouble with God for doing that but don't think for a second I didn't try to reason with God to get His permission just a couple of times. Since I couldn't bring myself to go against God, I don't have boobs today.

Once I was off alcohol, drugs and sex, I was left with just me. Who was I without all my coping mechanisms? Truthfully I didn't have a clue. As I learned how to live in my body without using my sexual nature, I felt lost.

To help me feel better about myself, I tanned constantly. God and I had many fights over my desire to go to the tanner. I didn't think I could be pretty without a nice brown color. I would obey Him for a while, and then rebel and go back to tanning. I finally agreed to do it His way for a few years and then re-addressed it with Him. This is what I heard, "You can go to the tanner but you will regret it." That was my green light. I went to the tanner twice that year and twice the next. I then got skin cancer and had to have a chunk of my leg and back removed.

As I continued to age, I started getting wrinkles and my skin wasn't nearly as tight as it used to be. After years of obsessing about how I looked and all my many flaws I thought I had, I started to believe if I wasn't pretty, I didn't have hope of being someone spectacular someday.

It was at that point, at 51 years old, that I took my diseased thinking to God and sought help. I confessed my crazy thoughts and asked what He wanted me to do about them. I felt Him encouraging me to focus on being beautiful on the inside. He then led me to read 1 Peter 3:3-5! What a revelation! I wanted so desperately to be beautiful on the outside but could care less about all the ugly qualities I possessed on the inside of me.

How do you feel about your looks?

____

____

____

What bothers you the most about your appearance?

____

____

____

What steps have you taken to fix what you dislike?

____

____

____

Have you taken your upset about your appearance to God? ______________________

If so, what do you think He said?

____

____

____

If not, why?

____

____

____

Would you be willing to write about everything you don't like about your appearance and give it all to God as an offering? Explain:

____

____

____

Are you willing to take whatever corrective action He shows you? __________________

It's your turn:

The need for healing!

..."See you are well! Sin no more, that nothing worst happens to you!"
John 5:14B ESV

Because I was a woman who could not behave, no matter how hard I tried, I was delighted when I met people who had the gifts of healing. I wanted to desperately be healed and whole so I could help other people get well.

Although God healed me through the years in a number of fashions, one of the first healing sessions I had was with one of the daughters of the special woman who took me in from the church that held the 'sex' class I attended. She was into 'deliverance' and since I had made that pact with the devil when I was 14, she was certain I needed her assistance to be free. I spent a lot of time with her and she prayed with me a lot. It was during this time that I felt the 'struggle was real' when it came to the spiritual realm. It truly felt like Satan was after my soul. My life was not easy to live because I was constantly being tormented.

The one thing she did for me was scare me about having sex. She told me once God set me free, I wouldn't want to have sex anymore because whatever my partner had, I could get. I figured I was bad enough on my own; I didn't need the help of anyone else so I tried desperately to behave myself in that area.

In what areas do you struggle to behave?

____

____

____

Do you have areas of your life that you are afraid to share for fear of that people may think?

____

As a result of my gut-wrenching honesty in this material, would you be willing to take a risk and dump your secrets? Why or why not:

____

____

____

Have you taken them to Jesus?

____

As I continued my journey toward wellness, I met the prayer pastor at the new church God led me to after my relapse. She was a conservative lady who was very loving and kind. She was very different from Grandma's daughter.

God saw fit to give me favor with the prayer pastor. She did healing sessions with me that really worked. I remember one that included prayer partners. They got scriptures when they prayed and gave them to me at the end of the session. I was supposed to study them but I never did. Perhaps this is why I struggled so.

It was this wonderful prayer pastor who prayed over me when I was having my difficulty with my 'friend' I almost married from the self-help meetings. God used her to set me straight.

Do you have people in your life who speak truth to you? ______________________________

Who are they?

____

____

____

What do you do when they tell you things you don't want to hear?

____

____

____

As I tried to become a better woman, I also worked the steps from the material at my self-help meetings. The combination of step work and healing prayer sessions really helped tremendously. I was starting to feel saner as time progressed. The other pieces of my life were starting to fall nicely into place as well.

Time went on and I hit another wall so I sought out healing again. I started realizing I loved God very much but didn't want anything to do with Jesus. It was as if He was a threat to my relationship with God. Unbeknownst to me, I had an issue with Jesus ever since I had relapsed. I blamed Him for my relapse...because I had tried to be religious and it didn't work. What the preachers had taught, I couldn't live up to so I blamed Him. I had this blackness within me that needed to be healed.

In my quest to get this resolved, I ended up going to a facility that did inner-healing prayer sessions. The man running the program was incredibly gifted in healing. I was so amazed by his abilities, I stayed and volunteered with him for a year. While I was there, God continued to show me areas in my life that needed to be addressed. As He brought things to my attention, I became better at letting Him in to do His healing work.

It was during this time God started teaching me about His love. I was so used to running to 'things' to make me feel good. I claimed God was so wonderful yet I didn't have the first clue how to let Him be the comforter of all my upsets. He wanted to be my Everything and He took the necessary time to show me that.

As my learning continued, I felt as though God just wanted me to sit with Him. I didn't have to say a word. It was in these quiet times God continued to heal me and make me whole. It was so wonderful to just be with Him and sit quietly in His love. His healing love was so intense, I spent large amounts of time basking in it.

Over time, I didn't want to do anything wrong because I was becoming a dear friend of His. The closer we grew, the more of my life I handed over to Him. Eventually, there was nothing He couldn't address with me because I wanted to be totally free. I knew I wouldn't be perfect but I wanted to be the best me possible and the only way I could do that was giving Him the different things He asked for.

Do you know how much God loves you? ____

How do you feel about God?

____

____

____

Do you believe He has a plan for your life? ________________________________

If you do, what do you think it is?

____

____

____

If you don't, why?

____

____

____

It's your turn:

The Makings of a Leader

*So let's not get tired of doing what is good.
At just the right time we will reap a harvest
of blessing if we don't give up.
Galatians 6:9 NLT*

After God captured my heart with His love, He led me to start a ministry for women so that I could share with them what He had shared with me. I was totally delighted at first. I wanted to immediately get out there and make a difference with all the women who had suffered like I had. God had other plans.

Over the course of three years, things moved incredibly slow. Why would He call me to ministry and then not let me go do it? Because He had more to do within me first. His healing continued and I had questions like: How can I be in ministry when I don't like some of His people? He had me alone for so long that I became very accustomed to it only being the two of us and my family. Life was pretty easy when that was the case.

It was questions like those that led me to another woman who does prayer sessions. God told me I had to go see her to address judgment. Judgement? Me, the gal who is supposed to be going into full time ministry, has to have prayer for judgment? I told God I did not want to go…and to that I heard, 'Yes, and a lot of people who need to see you don't want to either…so go!' WOW! That was direct!

I made my appointment and did as I was instructed. The session totally didn't go as I had anticipated. When we started praying, God took me back to being adopted. There was a ton of judgment around that because my mom was supposedly a teen from a 'religious' home.

According to what I was shown in that prayer session, I had lived my life detached from everyone and had no idea. When I looked back over my life, I felt as though I had wandered for the last 40 years without staying connected to people. I was married and had bouts of closeness with my husband but didn't feel closely connected to him all the time. I would get connected with the people in the groups I had done at church but when they were over, so was the closeness of the relationships. The only one I really felt close to was God. I was absolutely blown away by this discovery.

Who are the people in your life that are the most meaningful?

____

____

____

If you are not close to people, why do you think that is?

____

____

____

Deep down, would you like to have meaningful relationships with women you can trust? Explain your answer:

____

____

____

When you think about you and God, how close would you say the two of you are? Explain:

____

____

____

Do you want to be closer to Him?

____

If so, what could you do to make that happen?

____

____

____

If not, Why?

____

____

____

As I waited for God to really let me serve the public, I got so discouraged because He seemed to take forever. He led me to read Esther and told me that while she was being beautified on the outside, He was beautifying me on the inside. As I have admitted previously, I could be a real ugly person sometimes especially when it came to patience. Traffic surely brought out the worst of me as did slow clerks.

As I continued my journey with God, He started showing me that the next leg of my journey is going to be all about relationships. As I said previously, it is incredibly easy to be nice when it is only God and your family. Think about it, how can a woman be called to full time ministry and not be able to function in the midst of people?

As I prepare for the next leg of my journey, I am highly aware that leaders are called to a higher standard than others. Am I somewhat scared that I won't cut it? I am sensitive to that possibility. I am also keenly aware that God did not bring me this far to let me fail. If I ever start thinking it was my power that brought me this far, I am doomed to failure.

I am also aware that a lot of people fall off the deep end after they become popular. I pray for God's favor and anointing all the time. I want to cross the finish line to hear "Well done, good and faithful servant!" If do not submit to His will, I will never get that privilege.

Do you think God has a special calling for you? ______________________________

If so, what do you think it is?

____

____

____

If you could do anything for Him, what would it be?

____

____

____

What is stopping you from doing it?

____

____

____

Remember how the LORD your God led you through the wilderness for these 40 years, humbling you and testing you to prove your character, and find out whether or not you would obey His commands.
Deuteronomy 8:2 NLT

It's your turn:

Money

The LORD will open the heavens, the storehouse of His bounty,
To send rain on your land in season and to bless all the work of your hands.
You will lend to many nations but will borrow from no one.
Deuteronomy 28:12 NIV

I made a lot of poor decisions with money. As a juvenile, I cashed some of my cousin's checks and ended up in trouble with the law. Soon thereafter, I was placed in jail and foster care.

My first husband wanted all my money for drugs and alcohol; I wasn't smart enough to tell him no. One of his friend's told me she was getting evicted so she needed me to cash a check for her. One check led to several and to other people cashing them. She was kind enough to give me some of the money. All was wonderful until one of the gals got arrested trying to cash one in the bank. Because my name was on some of the checks, I took the blame. I then had to pay $3000+ in restitution and fines. I really believed I was doing her a favor because she had a husband and kids and then I ended up getting slammed with the consequences!

As time went on, I got a job as a waitress. It was wonderful because I had money every day I worked. I could spend it on whatever I wanted because I would always get more the next day. As my addiction progressed, so did the amount of money I spent on alcohol and drugs.

Through my 20s, I worked and blew my money. I had no concept of its value. I was with my wealthy boyfriend but he did not share his money with me. Perhaps that is why he had so much of it. I would ask for dresses and when he refused to buy them for me, I would call my sugar daddy to take me shopping.

Once I stopped waitressing, I had to learn how to manage my money because I only got paid a few times a month. I would go on shopping sprees with my daughter and blow a few hundred dollars at a time. This left us with barely enough money to survive. Unfortunately, this pattern continued for a number of years. I hated it because I couldn't seem to get above the poverty line.

When I was about 30, I took my income taxes for a couple of years and paid off the small amount of debt I had. At 32 years old, I was debt free! I wanted to celebrate by taking my income tax check, my daughter and my friend's car to Florida for Spring Break. We lived it up for the first time ever and spent almost all of our few thousand dollars.

Just days before our trip, I met my soon to be husband. I knew he was going to be my savior in many ways. We didn't talk about money so I didn't know what to expect. When we bought our wedding rings, we put them on the new line of credit we opened. For whatever reason, I went from being so proud of being debt free to feeling like it was totally alright to use credit. It was almost like it made me a liberated individual.

Because of all the financial abuse that has happened to me in the past, my husband allowed me to do all of the finances. He didn't check on me to be sure I was paying everything because he trusted me.

God tried to direct me financially. I went to Financial Peace University near the beginning of our marriage. That was a good program but I wasn't about to apply it to my life. When I overspent our cash on hand, I thought nothing of using the credit card despite what was taught in the class. As my appetites grew, so did the balances.

One day I felt God directing me to put our house on the market. I told my husband God wanted us to sell the house so we needed to do some updates. Although we were frivolous with our spending, we were on a 12-year mortgage with only six years left to pay.

Fast forward to $16-18,000 in home repairs and a market crash; we finally got the house on the market. When God told me to sell it, it was valued at $103,000 but because we waited, we sold it for $69,000. I was sick over what happened. What do you suppose went so terribly wrong? God didn't tell me to update it; He told me to sell it! Because I didn't listen to His direction, we paid tremendously!

Did your parents teach you about money? ____________________________________

Were you able to start your adult life on solid ground financially? ____________________

What did that look like?

____

____

____

How are you with money now?

____

____

____

What is your opinion of credit cards?

____

____

____

Do you think God cares how you use your money? Explain:

___

___

___

Those who love money will never have enough.
How meaningless to think that wealth brings true happiness.
Ecclesiastes 5:10 NLT

It's your turn:

What will it take?

It is senseless to pay to educate a fool,
Since he has no heart for learning.
Proverbs 17:16

We finally found a new place to live. It badly needed carpeting. Instead of asking God how He would handle it, I took out a line of credit and bought new carpet. I had this terrible feeling on the inside of me...you know that feeling...that 'God wants to talk to you about the decision you are about to make' feeling. I was so used to putting the other house repairs on the credit card; I did the same with the carpet. The only good part is I bought it on a zero interest account and had it paid before the due date. Looking back, I wonder how God would have handled it.

Because we lived like there was no tomorrow, we didn't save money for a down payment. This poor decision caused us to have to pay PMI insurance for the last seven years. That is equivalent to throwing a $100 bill in the toilet each month.

As the years went by, I started hating how much we owed between the credit cards and my student loans. As a quick fix against our accountant's advice, we cashed in a good part of my husband's IRA. We paid off my student loans, the credit cards and took about a $20,000 hit on the IRA...not to mention the extra taxes we had to pay because of it. After the fact, we learned I would have qualified for the student loan forgiveness program because I had been paying for ten years and had been working for the government. This was another financial mistake we made because we thought we knew best.

We weren't debt free for three days and I immediately charged airline tickets to Alaska for the family. I then had to battle to get them paid. As my balance would go down, something else would peak my interest and go on the card. I used it as my savior to get those things I thought I must have.

Thankfully God is an incredibly patience God. He finally had me stop using the credit cards and then the debit card (for the most part). He wanted me to learn how to use cash so I could understand the value of money. I would take out $150 for groceries, spend it and then go to the bank to get more money. This pattern continued for a while until I realized that was an unhealthy habit that caused us to run out of money before the end of the month. I would go to garage sales or Goodwill and overspend which resulted in my family having fewer groceries for the week. Sometimes I would spend the money and then have my husband use his debit card as if it did not count as my using it.

Christmas was a holiday I hated for many years. I always felt poor and unable to buy gifts for those I loved. Because 'gifts' is one of my love languages, it was a strong desire of mine to be able to participate. I could have prepared like some families; however, I chose instead to act like it had snuck up on me every year.

During my years of credit card abuse, I would act as though I had money and buy gifts using credit. I always promised to pay with the 3rd check of the month but because I was so undisciplined, I always carried the balance into the New Year. God finally asked me how many times I planned to go around the same mountain before I learned my lesson.

This past year, I felt led to buy a van for ministry purposes before I had sold my car. Because I had good credit, I took out a 2nd loan for the van. I paid off the car with the credit card to clear the title so I could sell it fast. God saw fit to let me make credit card payments on the car for three months before He sold it. That took me into December which again impacted my Christmas. Thankfully, He finally sold the car and I was able to enter the New Year without Christmas debt on the credit card.

Having the amount of the car on the credit card made me not want to buy any Christmas presents for anyone so I went into another Holiday season not celebrating the real reason for the season!

For security purposes, I like to keep a few hundred dollars in my checking account that is not recorded as my safety net. As I was sitting in a church service that December, God impressed on my heart to give my cushion away to pay someone's rent. Was He kidding? No. He was not kidding; He was very serious and I knew it. So I walked to the guest counter and left a check for the gal who needed her rent paid. Was I bawling? You better bet I was. That was my security, my safety net and now God was asking me to totally trust Him to be my security.

When it comes to money, what has God asked you to do that was painful?

____

____

____

Did you do it? ____

How did you feel after the fact?

____

____

____

How do you feel about regular tithing?

____

____

____

Do you understand if you give God your first fruits, He will make sure your needs are met? What are those needs?

____

____

____

Bring the whole tithe into the storehouse, that there may be food in my house.
Test me in this, says the LORD Almighty. And see if I will not throw
Open the floodgates of heaven and pour out so much blessing
That there will not be room enough to store it.
Malachi 3:10

It's your turn:

Money doesn't buy happiness!

Keep your lives free from the love of money
And be content with what you have
Because God has said,
"Never will I leave you; never will I forsake you."
Hebrews 13:5 NIV

For years I believed if I only made more money, our lives would be wonderful. As our salaries continued to grow, so did the expenses. We were making more money than ever but it felt like we had less to spend. It was during this time that I felt God telling me to quit my job and go into full time ministry.

Being the spenders we were, we didn't tuck away a nest egg for the future. The last month I got three paychecks, we felt God lead us to put most of the 3rd check into the building projects at church. I didn't challenge God at all; I did as He instructed confident He would meet my needs as they arose.

Being a woman who likes to know she is going to be taken care of, God has brought me amazing peace. My last paycheck was the equivalent of 3 weeks' pay. I paid all of our bills for the month and we have been careful with how we live. I felt God told me not to be worried about it and not to live recklessly. I have followed His guidance and all has been well.

This new journey is a leap of faith because my husband doesn't make enough money to pay all of our bills. Thankfully we have been making double vehicle payments so we can skip those for a bit if need be. We also don't have to make our daughter's tuition payment for two months in the summer so that has been a bonus.

I prayed for money for school clothes and supplies as well as to be able to take my husband on a 19-year wedding anniversary trip for a couple of days. God provided the money to take my girl school shopping for both clothes and supplies. He also had a very dear friend write me a check for $500 to take my man away to celebrate our anniversary. He then had another gal provide a nice home on Lake Charlevoix for a very reasonable price.

Because I can still get lost trying to solve my own problems, I was out walking my dogs one-day fretting about how I was going to get my daughter her school shoes she needed. I then heard, "Why don't you ask Me for the money for the shoes?" I could have whacked myself in the head for that one! "Oh yes God, how am I going to get the money for my girl's shoes?" I then walked to the mail box and found a $167 check. I was so excited that God came through for my girl and me. She too was excited when I was able to pick her up from camp and take her shopping at her favorite Outlet Stores.

I believed with all of my heart God told me if I left my job, He would give me a promotion. I worked there 15 years, made decent money, had seven weeks of vacation and 13.5 holidays. None of that mattered if I was miserable. When I realized I was living for my days and weekends off, I knew something had to change.

What I have learned in the last two months is we can live on a lot less than we think we can. As I said previously, we made more than we ever had yet I felt like we had less. Granted, we were making double payments on our vehicles and paying for supplements to take care of our health which were very expensive.

I don't know where my next money is coming from but I know I have a very close relationship with God. I have been home writing this workbook and have been happier than I have been in a very long time. He has had me on a healing journey showing me ways I have been stuck in bondage for years. Since I left my job, I have not gone without one thing I have needed.

Trust in the Lord with all of your heart and
do not lean on your own understanding,
in all your ways acknowledge Him and
He will make your paths straight.
Proverbs 3:5-6 ESV

Are you happy at your current job? ____

If you could do anything, what would it be?

____

____

____

When it comes to money, what has God asked you to do out of the ordinary?

____

____

____

Have you done it? ____

What was the outcome?

____

____

____

Many years ago, I couldn't figure out what I could possibly do with my life because I didn't think I had potential. I then started to ask God what He thought I would be good at doing. He gave me a vision of doing exactly what I hope to do at my new position. I saw myself working with women in both group and individual sessions. When this happened, I became ALIVE because I knew I could do what He showed me. I just needed to do the footwork.

If you could have your dream job, what would it be?

____

What steps do you need to take in order to make it happen?

____

____

____

If you do not know what you want to do, I want you to sit with God and ask Him to clearly show you why you are here on this earth. Use your journaling space to document what He shows you.

It's your turn:

Alive at Last Ministries

For the LORD your God is bringing you into a good land of flowing streams and pools of water, with fountains and springs that gush out of the valleys and hills…it is a land where food is plentiful and nothing is lacking…
Deuteronomy 8: 7,9a

Even though my heart was set on full time ministry, I would sometimes still try to figure things out on my own. I had hoped to start the ministry at the church we had been attending for a couple years. Thankfully God finally showed me that was not going to happen. He asked me to trust Him and moved us twice before we landed back at the church we had left ten years earlier. We started back in a leadership group. God told me I couldn't do ministry for the entire nine weeks of the class. On the 8th week, one of the gals in the group asked if she could write a check to start the ministry. It was amazing…but I didn't feel the incredibleness I felt I should have experienced.

When I asked God about it, I felt He told me it was because I didn't know how to let Him love me big. Interesting. Just before this happened, I had taken a trip with my husband to celebrate our 18th anniversary. We have always enjoyed garage saleing on the way to our destinations. At one of the sales, I bought the book "He Speaks to Me" by Priscilla Shirer.

I was so excited to get the book and started reading it immediately. One of the things the author asked in the first chapter was whether we are willing to obey God. Yikes! It was at that moment in our motel room that God opened my eyes to something that was troubling Him. He nailed me for using my debit card and said I was being sneaky.

As I pondered how much I hated the word, I had to look at my behavior. Was I being sneaky? I used the card to book our room (knowing He did not want me to use it) instead of asking how He wanted me to handle it. As much as I said I wanted to be close to God and give Him everything, there were still areas of my life where I took matters into my own hands…and this was one of them.

He does say in His word that unless we become like the little children, we don't get to inherit the kingdom of God…I am positive being sneaky like a little child is NOT what He had in mind.

Over the next couple months, God poured His love out on me as I read and reread that book. I wanted to be everything He called me to be so I could help whoever He brought to me…and I needed to be on point because now He had given me the money to officially start the ministry.

Much to my dismay, it was another eight months before He really busted the doors open and let me see clients. I had a small group at the office but I wanted to see people. I wanted to change lives…and as I drew closer and closer to Him, I felt like I was again stuck in that long lonely corridor.

As the weeks continued to pass, our church kept singing the song 'Do it again' by Elevation Worship. I would absolutely bawl as I sang it because I most certainly thought the walls should have fallen long before now. It was at one of those Sunday services; I had the privilege of officially meeting our pastor. One thing led to another and I was able to have a meeting with him and let him know about the ministry. It was the beginning of God breaking ground for me to start seeing clients.

When Spring Break neared, I felt strongly that I was not to schedule anything for myself. I was pumped because I knew God had something special planned for me. All of a sudden, my ministry line started ringing. God had me start seeing clients and it was amazing. I was walking on water with excitement. God was finally using me. On the 9th day of my break, God had me read a book that one of my past board members had written. It was the story of her life and all the abuse she had suffered. I was floored by what I read. I realized I didn't have a clue she had undergone such torment...and if that happened to her, who else had been so unfortunate?

As soon as I was done with the book, I felt led to get on my knees and start praying. It was during that prayer time; God directed me to go to work and give my notice. I was to be done on June 1st so I could go into full time ministry. I was absolutely elated that the day was finally coming. I now had seven weeks and I would be working full time for God.

As I worked toward my resignation date, I was struggling to see myself doing life without my participants. I had been in that job for 15 years. I never realized what an asset I was there until it was time to depart. I had spent the last few years being lost in my boredom unable to see the work that could have been done to keep me engaged.

About the middle of May, I found myself getting very upset that they hadn't hired someone. Because of my overdeveloped sense of responsibility, I agreed to stay on but I was not happy about it. In fact, I found myself very angry...questioning God. As I was telling God what I thought, I heard, "You act like I did not know this was going to happen!" As I thought about it, I realized He was absolutely right. I acted like He didn't know! How could someone who claims she wants to work full time for God not realize He knew this was going to happen all along?

As far as my job was concerned, I reached the point where I didn't want to look for the things that were wrong with the ladies on my caseload. I wanted to try to help the ones who wanted to get better figure out how to make that happen. The last few weeks on my job were somewhat excruciating because of that. I found myself mad because my boss wanted me to do a job I was no longer interested in doing. At that point, I tried the best I could to be nice as I served out the rest of my time.

When I was finally done with my job, I took the rest of the week off to unwind. I had been working full time and still seeing clients on the side. My weeks had been full for three months and I was tired. I felt like God told me I would take July and have a sabbatical of sorts with Him. I was to draw close in preparation for what was next. It was during this time I felt He wanted me to write my story.

As I drew close to Him and enjoyed my new life, I spent a lot of time writing. I felt like I was supposed to be very honest about my life as He brought subjects to mind. I then questioned Him to make sure I was doing what He wanted. Is my story really going to help anyone? It was then He said it was His story of my redemption that is going to help people.

What have you waited for God to do in your life?

What did you do in the meantime?

What do you most want Him to heal?

It's your turn:

After all these years?

The thief comes only to steal and kill and destroy;
I have come that they may have life and have it to the full.
John 10:10 NIV

A few weeks into my new journey of full time ministry, God brought up a topic that caught me totally off guard. Many times through the years I mentioned I had been molested by my grandfather and believed wholeheartedly it did not have an impact on me. I was sure my daddy leaving our family was what had devastated me. The last memory I have of my dad being in our house was when he put his arms around me to say good bye. I thought for sure he was going to touch my breast like my grandfather did and I cringed at the very thought of it. When I think back to that moment, I have no recollection of his words, only what he might have done to me.

Fast forward 41 years to my life today. What a surprise when God brought it to my attention that He wanted to address that abuse. I was totally floored...but like everything else He showed me, I wanted the truth so I could be free.

In His loving way, He showed me I lost my voice when the abuse took place. I didn't like what happened to me but I never told him to stop nor did I tell my mom or my grandma. For whatever sick reason, it continued to happen and I didn't say a word. It wasn't that I liked it, I just didn't know how to I tell him to stop.

Hours have been spent over the last several weeks doing this writing project. It astounds me to believe I am the same woman as the one I wrote about in these pages. It is absolutely heartbreaking to think of the things I allowed numerous men to do to me without my objecting. Often I didn't like what was being done to me but I allowed it to continue anyhow. I really had to be broken before I would stand up for myself and do something different. Thankfully the day finally came when I started to get sick of being other people's sperm banks and started to say no.

In the process of wrapping up my writing project, I asked God why He brought the repression of sexual abuse to my attention when He did. I have been on a quest to get well for a number of years, why now?

As I sat quietly to hear what He had to say, I felt He said it was time for me to know the truth. It was time for me to know why I stayed in all those situations of abuse. I thought I wasn't smart enough to escape. My problem didn't have anything to do with brains...it was about losing my voice when I was ten and not knowing it.

Unlike what it may have done to some, my new found information didn't devastate me. It actually liberated me. It opened my eyes to the fact that I do indeed have a voice and I don't have to let other people make my decisions anymore. Just because people want something doesn't mean I have to give in to them.

I also get to launch my new career as a healed and whole woman chosen by God to love and cherish other women who have had similar pasts. I get to teach them that we don't have to tolerate abuse in any fashion. We are all God's chosen daughters and He doesn't like it when people hurt us. He also doesn't like it when we continue to tolerate being hurt.

God has an incredible future planned for each and every one of us. The question then becomes are we going to take the time to find out what it is or are we going to continue living the lives we are today? He is not the least bit afraid of messy...in fact He specializes in it. He then calls those He has healed to be shining examples that redemption is possible for all of us...not just a select few.

What do you think is left for God to heal?

____

____

____

What areas of your life are you refusing to give Him?

____

____

____

What would it take for you to surrender?

____

____

____

I can honestly tell you there is not one area of my life God cannot have. I do not say that to brag, I say it to celebrate. What He is now doing is teaching me how to live up to my calling.

He has now called me to be the executive director of Alive at Last Ministries. You have read where I have come from so hopefully, you can understand some of the inner conflict I have experienced at the thought of it. ME, an executive director?!

Please note: I am the one who has continually said, "God, I will do whatever you ask." He is clearly asking me to do this for Him. Is it way over my head? Yes. Am I afraid? Yes. Will I do it? Yes.

This is why: God is not going to lead me to do something and then expect me to do it myself. He is going to walk every step of the way with me just like He has the last 51 years of my life. The difference between now and then is that I am much more cognoscente of His Presence today. When I feel Him directing me, I am much quicker to respond. I also realize I don't have to live up to anyone else's idea of an executive director; I have to live up to what He wants me to be.

When I think about how intellectual and conservative some of the executive directors are I have met, there is no way I could compete. In the midst of my comparing myself to some of them, I felt God ask if I thought people like that could help the population of women I have been called to help. The answer was a quick NO! Not at all!

God has called me to be authentic and genuine. He also wants me to be loving and caring. I can do that. I can be honest about who I am and dedicated to helping every woman He brings to me for help. I want to grow into all He has called me to become without forgetting all the treacherous roads it has taken me to get here.

This is the best part of my whole story: God doesn't love me any more than He loves you. What He has done for me, He will do for you. He has exciting adventures planned for you just like He does for me. He wants to heal everywhere you hurt so you too can be a shining example of His incredible redemption.

With that said, what do you want to say to God?

____

____

____

____

____

____

____

It's your turn:

The Triathlon

I hear the Lord saying, "I will stay close to you,
instructing and guiding you along the pathway for your life.
I will advise you along the way
and lead you forth with my eyes as your guide.
So don't make it difficult; don't be stubborn
when I take you where you've not been before.
Don't make me tug you and pull you along.
Just come with me!"
Psalm 32:8 and 9

Ready to conquer the world after resigning from my 15-year career, I talked a friend into joining a local triathlon with me. I had prayed about which training group to attend several times, and I continually felt like I was supposed to join the Wednesday evening group.

My friend and I showed up to the first group, and we could tell it seemed a bit cliquey. I had just driven in from Mackinac City with a van full of 6th graders, so I was ready for some adult interaction and exercise.

I wanted to meet some new people and thought this would be the perfect opportunity. Little did I know, God had a whole lot more planned than just my meeting people and getting some exercise.

Have you ever joined a local group for exercise? ______________________________
What was that like for you?

____

____

____

What kind of groups would you like to join?

____

____

____

As the weeks went by, I could feel the loneliness of being rejected by my leaders/women in the clique. If I wouldn't have had my friend there, I would have surely quit. The leader was so obsessed with her own training; she could care less about any of the rest of us...unless they were part of her special group.

The straw that broke the camel's back was when a few of us went to the tire changing workshop (a bonus perk for the Tri). She came in late and stood by me and didn't even say hello. Her behavior totally baffled me and left a very nasty feeling deep within me. What was so wrong with me that she couldn't acknowledge my presence? Had I done something to offend her?

I wanted to do well and finish in one piece so my friend and I tried to practice three days a week. They had a special swimming group one Tuesday evening so I attended. The group welcomed me and was very endearing. She and I also joined the Friday group one morning, and they were even more loving and caring than the Tuesday group. There was a gal at the back of the bike group to make sure no one felt left out or behind. Imagine the love the ladies in her group felt!

After having had this experience with the Friday group, I really questioned why God would have put me in the Wednesday night group knowing how my friend and I were going to be treated. What on earth was I supposed to learn from this lesson?

When is the last time you were led to do something and the result was not what you had anticipated?

____

What did you learn from the experience?

____

____

____

How did you feel about God as a result of the experience?

____

____

____

As I continued to let this eat at me, I began acting in a juvenile fashion. My flesh was getting the best of me and I started talking bad about our leaders with the other people who felt the same way I did. I really let them get the best of me as I continued to live in the problem.

How do you respond when you are in troubling situations where you feel helpless?

____

____

____

Are you a person who talks behind someone's back and never confronts the problem or do you like to confront the problem head on and get it resolved? ______________________________

How do you think this has impacted you and your relationships?

____

____

____

The big race day came and I could see the groups of people there to support each other. Not our group though. There was the clique and all the outsiders who weren't included! The funny thing was, they invited us to the after party later that evening. Needless to say, neither my friend nor I joined them.

It wasn't until all the hoorah was over that God began to show me what the real problem was. I had been proud of the fact that I didn't have a problem with rejection...that is, until it smacked me in the face during this triathlon.

One morning as I sat in my office totally lost, God showed me I had tons of rejection in my life; I just wouldn't take the time to acknowledge it. It was then that He started giving me visual flashbacks of different times I was left out of situations. He showed me visions of middle school and how I was left out and lost. I didn't know how to connect with the other kids because of the unaddressed trauma actively unfolding in my life. It was then that I started shutting people out of my life and turning to unhealthy behaviors to anesthetize my brokenness.

After getting a grasp of what was really wrong with me, I felt like I should make amends for gossiping behind the leader's back and putting in a bad review. I tried to meet with the leader and she stood me up. I then went to the grocery store. and who did I run into but the leader of the group. Sure enough, God had me stand right there in the parking lot and discuss how upset I was about the whole situation. She noted she forgot about the meeting and was apologetic for her behavior, not realizing or intending it to hurt anyone.

Doing what God asked didn't heal me from being rejected but it did shine a light on my own unhealthy behaviors when I feel hurt and act out in unbecoming ways.

Have you ever felt like you were rejected? ____

If so, how did you handle the situation?

____

____

____

How are you a different person today because of it?

____

____

____

It's your turn:

Oh the Beloved Wilderness

Without realizing what was happening, my poor choices created yet another incredible mess. Once again I allowed chocolate to engulf my wellbeing. It impacted the intimacy between God and I, but I was so ticked at Him, I didn't care. I was too busy making a mess of everything I touched to stop long enough to seek His guidance on the issue. It didn't matter to me that it was the HOLY SEASON...I was a miserable woman and I was going to do whatever it took to bring myself a little bit of joy, even if it cost me what I said I valued most in life. Unfortunately, the more chocolate I ate, the more enjoyment I experienced.

You see, I had ideals of what I thought my life should look like. I quit my job to serve this so called King of the Universe. I gave up a decent salary, a lot of vacation, several paid holidays, not to mention health insurance. When I first did it, it wasn't a big deal. He kept me busy writing this workbook and training for my triathlon, I was a pretty content woman.

Then came the days when the bills started rolling in and my husband's salary was not enough to pay all of them. I would have thought I had learned to sit quietly and seek His face before jumping into the deep waters of full dependence upon Him, but I obviously had not. Here I was, a woman wanting others to fully trust in God, all the while I am quickly sinking into my own pit of despair because I didn't know how to do it myself.

So what did this supposed 'fully devoted follower of Christ' do in the midst of her gut-wrenchingly traumatic situation? I started throwing a whole lot more than fits. Cuss words were flying, and I was so angry, I felt like I could rip God to shreds if He would have only gotten down here so we could physically fight in person.

What do you do when life does not go as you anticipate it will?

____

____

____

How often do you take out your upset on God? ________________________________

You see, satan worked overtime trying to get me to hate God and not trust Him. As I continued to listen to his lies, the more venomous I became. Poison was spewing from my lips as if I worked for the devil rather than God. The saddest part of this story is that I was leading a bible study about the Armor of God. Here I was, a seasoned Christian of decades, sinking in the mire of the deceit of the very enemy we were supposed to be learning how to defeat.

The unfortunate news is I spent months in the very pit I helped the enemy dig for me. I pulled out my zero balance credit card and started charging it up…all the while saying, "If GOD can't take care of me, my Visa card will!" Hating to admit the truth, months went by as I continued to wallow in this pit of despair.

Do you self-sabotage when things don't go your way? ______________________________

How do you feel after the fact?

____

____

____

How long does it take you to make your way back to God after you get upset with Him?

____

The pressure to give up and do it a different way was so intense I thought I was going to explode…when in actuality, I did, every chance I got. I could have cared less what people thought. I was a very miserable woman, and I wasn't afraid to talk about it.

To make matters worse, one of my friends suggested I do what others would do in my situation…get a job. That statement absolutely infuriated me. Are you kidding me? Do you not think I am close enough to God to know if He wants me to get a job? I asked over and over if I could get a job. Do you know what I heard? "I gave you a job!" To that I responded, "I do love my job…I just hate that I am not getting paid to do it."

You see, He was starting to bring me a few clients. To my initial delight, they had Blue Cross insurance which was supposed to pay very well. The problem was their employers contracted with other agencies so I did NOT get paid at all for several months because I was not affiliated with them. When I finally got paid, it was only a fraction of what it was supposed to be.

Because I was so miserable, I absolutely gorged myself with chocolate. It was the perfect buzz. I knew God didn't want me doing it, and I knew it impacted the intimacy between us, but I could have cared less. He knew I was a broken mess and didn't seem to care. Why should I care about what He wanted?

My birthday came so I decided to go shopping and out to a fancy dinner. I didn't have any problem living it up on my Visa card. God hadn't done anything to see to it that it was a special day for me. Later that evening, I called a close friend of mine and absolutely fell apart. She didn't know what to do with all the hatred I had toward God for not taking care of me.

The saddest part of all of this was I didn't ask God how He wanted me to handle my lack of finances. I was so angry He wasn't letting me make money and support myself. I kept screaming, "What do you want me to do?" I kept hearing, "just be". What? How in the world am I supposed to survive 'just being'? 'Be still and know that I am God' was His answer.
As angry as I was, the last thing I wanted to do was be still with a God who would make me face my worst fear: going without enough money to pay my bills. If I knew I could have gone and gotten a job and been successful without His help, I would have done it in an instant. Where I was stuck was that I believed I would never be successful without His help, and so I had to suffer it out and follow where He led, kicking and screaming the whole way.

Thankfully God used people to come through with money to help meet our needs a few different months. It always shocked me to see the miracle appear after another of my crying rants.

How has God come through when you needed it the most?

____

____

____

Have you had to experience facing your worst fears? ___________________________

What was it like for you?

____

____

____

Despite what an uncontrolled brat I had been for the last several months, God had a special treat for me. A friend of mine bought a copy of this workbook and was incredibly touched by it. She had just been given a Christmas bonus from her job so she called to see what I needed. I told her my debacle about the insurance companies and how much I thought I was going to get paid and didn't. The next morning, she met me with a check for $600 and a brand new Michael Kors computer bag. This was truly God in action. I felt loved for a few days...but that didn't stop me from overdosing on chocolate right through the holidays.

What are you doing right now that you know God doesn't want you doing?

____

____

____

If He were here with you right now, what do you think He would say to you about it?

____

____

____

What would you like to say to Him about it?

____

____

____

Behold, I am standing at the door knocking. If your heart is open
To hear my voice and you open the door within,
I will come in to you and feast with you and you will feast with me.
Rev.3:20 TPT

It's your turn:

It's time to surrender

Behold, I am standing at the door knocking. If your heart is open
To hear my voice and you open the door within,
I will come in to you and feast with you and you will feast with me.
Rev.3:20 TPT

On January 1, 2019, I was a broken mess. I had wasted half of the previous year overdosing on chocolate because it made me high and helped me deal with the misery of supposedly being in ministry. That morning, God clearly asked me to surrender the chocolate and give Him a chance to do something with the horrible disaster I felt I had become.

Following that I had a vision of myself as a hollow individual who didn't have a clue who she was. I looked into the future and saw absolutely nothing. I didn't have any clients on the books. I had money that was supposed to come from insurance companies, but no matter what I did it wasn't coming. There I was...STUCK! I was supposed to be working for God but I was so disillusioned. I actually hated my life. I didn't trust His provision because our credit card continued to escalate. I was a blank canvas, lost, questioning everything about my existence. Truly, I saw no hope for my future. I didn't trust God and I totally despised this supposed calling I had on my life!

Our church did a fast in January. I really wanted to believe God was going to do a major breakthrough during that time. The topic was about the Promised Land. I came home from one of the sessions and felt led to write about what I thought my Promised Land would look like.

My 'Promised Land' would consist of having enough money to pay my bills (not having to depend on God to supply), a nice home, a shiny car, money in the bank. You know, all the things the happy people have.

What would your 'Promised Land' look like?

____

____

____

What do you think you need right now to be happy?

____

____

____

The special time of fasting came and went and I did not have a breakthrough, at least not one that I recognized. I continued to wallow in my pit of despair wondering when God was going to do something to make this nightmare I was living come to a screeching halt.

On February 1, 2019 around 5:00 pm, I sent word to a couple people that I was quitting the ministry because God didn't supply the money I needed to pay for my office. How could I possibly tell my clients God would take care of them if He couldn't even take of me when I gave up everything to serve Him?

One of the gals I notified, who I walked with through the last few years, panicked and offered to give me the money needed to balance my budget for the month. She talked about how much I had helped her and she couldn't imagine me not being able and available to help others. To test my faith further, God then allowed me to make a whopping $20 in February.

The early months of 2019 were excruciating. God spent time lovingly leading me to open up places within me that I had no idea needed healing. He used the down time when I didn't have clients to take me back to my childhood and all the hurt I had stuffed. He exposed traumatic things to me that I had no idea existed. He showed me the little girl who was devastated and how she proceeded to deal with it the last 40 years of her life. I had totally been oblivious to how I disconnected from all that hurt and pain. I had erected walls that were super thick to prevent people from getting close to me.

As God continued to heal me, He also started opening doors for me. I went to a Joyce Meyer conference and felt led to plant all the money I had received from seeing one of my few clients into the offering plate as seed for the ministry. I did just that and was utterly amazed when my seed started to grow, He started bringing me regular clients.

About midsummer, I felt led to plan a family vacation to celebrate my 20th wedding anniversary. We went up north and stayed at a family friend's cottage by the lake. It was a wonderful trip.

Are you able to see the ways God wants to bless you? ______________________________

When is the last time He did something special for you? ____________________________

What did He do?

____

____

____

Do you have any idea how much He wants to lavish His love upon you and do special things for you?

____

How do you feel when you think about that?

___

___

___

God continued to prove He had things under control as He proceeded to bring me regular clients. I truly believe He wanted me to build the practice so I could support the ministry. He also allowed me to use the money to pay off the credit card I had been using while waiting for my breakthrough.

As I continued to learn how to trust Him, my life unfolded in amazing ways. I became more healed and whole. I began to experience emotional and financial stability. The things I thought I couldn't be happy without the previous year really didn't matter now. I just wanted to experience peace and happiness.

As 2019 came to a close, I had only made $13,000 for the year but I was happier than I had ever been. I was finally learning how to live the adventure I was called to live. It didn't matter how old I was, what mattered is what I was helping others find the same freedom I had discovered. The more I invested in others, the more I felt freedom from the bondage of self.

Where do you still feel bound? ___

What do you think it would take to finally surrender?

___

___

___

What dreams do you have that have yet to take place?

___

___

___

As I have continued to watch the adventure unfold, I felt like God was asking me to start dreaming again. What would that look like? After being eaten alive by satan in late 2018, I came out of that experience beaten and bloodied. My self-worth and self-esteem were very delicate. I spent time with God and tried to follow where He led but I was extremely timid due to being internally striped and recreated.

As God continued to heal me, I realized I missed out on a lot of things as a young girl and young adult. Due to all the abuse, I lost my voice and much more. I missed out on many things regular people get to do, such as dreaming about a new house and a nice car. Looking back, my life was nothing but a series of bad decisions. Had God not intervened, I wouldn't be alive to tell of the miracle that He truly is the God who meets the woman on the bar stool and wherever else she finds herself in disarray.

Can you see God doing something spectacular with your mistakes? ____________________

How do you think your mistakes could benefit others? ____________________

Would you be willing to invite Him in to showcase His grace? ____________________

As a special surprise, my friend invited me to her home on Marco Island in Florida. It was an amazing trip that opened my eyes to the true wonder of God. The place was incredible. I had felt God tell me I needed to get ready for a retreat and that is exactly what is was. My friend made me delicious meals as we enjoyed our time together. We weren't racing to see all the sites; we were simply basking in His presence enjoying the wonder of His creation.

The best part of that story is I could totally be me amidst all that wealth and not feel like I needed it or had to have it for myself. I was able to be immensely blessed by it and not covet what once could have ruined me. Obviously God knew this would be exactly what I needed to kick off 'Advent' in nothing shy of amazement. What a way to celebrate the positive choices I had made in 2019.

As for any of you who think God doesn't bless our obedience, I have photos to prove otherwise!

Again I ask: What is He asking you to surrender? ____________________

*If you bow low in God's awesome presence,
He will eventually exalt you as you leave the
timing in His hands. Pour out all your worries and
stress upon Him and leave them there,
for He always tenderly cares for you.
1 Peter 5:6 & 7 TPT*

It's your turn:

Are you sure you want to search me?

God, I invite your searching gaze into my heart.
Examine me through and through;
find out everything that may be hidden within me,
Put me to the test and sift through all my anxious cares.
Psalms 139: 23 & 24

As I became more cozy and comfortable with God and His love, I started getting more serious about wanting to be a top notch individual. In my quest, I started asking Him to search me and test my anxious thoughts. After all, no one knows me like He does.

In the past that prayer was said very sparingly! I only prayed it when I was feeling super spiritual...and there was enough distance from the last time that I forgot what happened when I had prayed it. Unbeknownst to me, I had a lot of unhealed emotions along with a lot of other things God wanted permission to address.

After I submitted my resignation at Drug Court, I truly felt as though I had lived through a living Hell. Between lack of trust and self-pity, I was openly a mangled mess. I felt like I had barely crawled out of all that alive. So when peace finally came, the last thing I really wanted to do was disturb it.

I found myself becoming very comfortable within the confines of my own home. It was very enlightening when He brought it to my attention what I started doing: I would go out to see clients and then hurry right back home where life felt safe.

The problem, I soon found, was that I had forgotten how to treat people when I had to interact with them for ordinary things. If I had to call an insurance company and they didn't tell me what I wanted to hear, I found myself getting very snarky. Heaven forbid how ugly I sounded if I couldn't understand the people because of their nationality. How about the poor service gal who had to tell me they didn't have the soup or bagel I wanted? Or what about the gals in the coffee shop standing there in the dark who told me they weren't opening today. "What do you mean you're not opening today?" I barked as if they were committing the unpardonable sin.

How do you treat people when they don't tell you what you want to hear?

____

____

____

You see, as I continued to draw close to God, He continued to show me the ugly places within me that would not be acceptable in the new places He was taking me. Just so you know, this has been a very uncomfortable experience!

The cozier I have become with Him, the gutsier I have gotten with my prayers. "Oh God, search me and show me anything that doesn't fit with my new life!" Being the faithful God He is, He does show us. Thankfully I have learned to stop making excuses for my incredulous behavior.

After I lit into the gals at the coffee shop that morning, unable to understand why they would be there if they weren't going to open, I went to God (after my friend brought my conduct to my attention) with my behavior. He kindly showed me that I expected to be served when in fact, He put me there to serve. Oh!

Hating to admit it, there were many little episodes that needed to be addressed. There was the whole mask issue thanks to COVID. I felt like I couldn't breathe in them so I did my best not to wear them.

A thought crossed my mind the evening before I went into a health food store: how I would respond should someone aggravate me? Sure enough, not 15 hours later, I was being put to the test. I walked into this store to grab my goodies. There were 3 checkout lanes. As I was jockeying for position, a controlling woman took it upon herself to tell me where the line was. Mind you, I am not from this city. I barked something to the effect that I was glad she made it her responsibility to tell me where to stand. The ponytailed male at the checkout then decided to light into me because I wasn't wearing my mask correctly. You can imagine my blood was boiling! Who was he to tell me how to wear my mask?

As I went to the next checkout lane, I decided I would not support a store that had treated me so poorly. The innocent cashier who tried to assist me suggested I speak with the managers on my way out of the store. At first I walked past but then went back and aired my grievances. Not feeling I was getting anywhere, I went to my vehicle to leave the parking lot. As I drove out of their only driveway, there stood the gal who aggravated me talking to the same managers. I had the privilege of driving right past them with my big 'Alive at Last Ministries' sticker on the back of the van.

Stewing, I went back to the hotel room to process all of this with God. I was appalled to be treated like this when I didn't even live in the area. As I was journaling my upset, you will never guess which scripture came to me: "As far as it depends on you, make it your ambition to live at peace with all people". "God, are you kidding me right now? That is all you have to say about the way I was just treated?" That was all He had to say. I knew there was no sense in pushing the issue! I failed yet again.

Have you ever had a situation like this take place?

____

____

____

This, like every other lesson, has taken time to learn. Unfortunately, I am still not 100%. My youngest daughter has a tender personality. Because I teach her to 'lead up', she now grabs my arm or shoots me a look if she feels I am acting in a way that is inconsistent with who I want to be. It is amazing who God uses to keep us on course!

Have you ever considered asking God to search your heart? ____________________________

If so, what was the result?

____

____

____

Thankfully I am comfortable enough with my family and some friends that I allow them to speak into my life. When my tone is off, they help me get it corrected. I never want to hurt anyone with the things I say. Hopefully those moments, when those closest to me point out my blind spots, are becoming fewer and farther between.

Who is in your life helping with your blind spots?

____

____

____

How do you handle your convictions when God points them out?

____

____

____

What do you do when you are confronted with unbecoming behaviors within yourself?

____

____

____

Do you believe God only brings them to our attention because they conflict with where He wants to take us? ____

How does that make you feel?

I am the sprouting vine and you are my branches.
As you live in union with me as your source,
Fruitfulness will stream from within you-
But when you live separated from me you are powerless.
John 15:5 TPT

It's your turn:

Oh how He loves Me!

You didn't choose me, but I've chosen and commissioned
you to go into the world to bear fruit.
And your fruit will last, because whatever you ask of my Father,
for my sake, He will give it to you!
So this is my parting command: Love one another deeply!"
John 15:16-17

As I look back over my life and see all the challenges of the addictions that have entangled me, it is utterly amazing that the God of the universe could or would even think of loving someone like me. As you have read, I hurt people. I manipulated and deceived them. I had abortions and slept with people from here to California while I was out hitchhiking. All this before I was saved and received my conscience.

And what about all the wrong I did after I met God but had no idea how to live according to my new life? What about all those mistakes? The thong bikinis, wild parties and all that filthy language that was deeply engrained in me? How about all the drug binges that kept rearing their ugly heads and destroying any progress I was able to make?

One could have looked at my supposed Christian life and made all kinds of mean comments and expressed all kinds of nasty statements. And some did. Everyone had their opinion and some of them were downright hateful.

So what about when I started letting God really work in my life? What about the days when I thought no one was as qualified as me to present the amazing abilities of God to a 12 Step meeting? The days when I was so full of pride and arrogance from being used by God that must have made Him sick to His stomach? How about the days when I became so legalistic and was downright hateful? How about when I became so engrossed in my own little world that I could care less if people I knew and supposedly loved were going to burn in Hell? Someone who got so sick of people I wanted no part of them because I let myself get burned out from lack of self-care?

How could a loving God even think of choosing someone like that to serve Him in His kingdom?

What do you think God thinks of you?

____

____

____

Do you have a hard time believing He loves you despite your flaws? ______________________

Thankfully God sees what we don't, and sometimes won't, see in others. He sees what we are going to be and He loves us accordingly. He distributes extraordinary amounts of grace which enables us to keep the course.

When we engage in a loving relationship with Him, He guides us to loving relationships that help us along our path to freedom. He places people and opportunities in our lives to get us to the next phase of our development.

Name one situation God has done for you that seemed like a miracle:

____

____

____

If we are open to His leading, He will lead us to jobs that we would never apply for or think we were qualified for.

What opportunities has God encouraged you to try despite feeling unworthy or unable?

____

____

____

As I continue to re-engage in society, it is amazing to hear what I would consider 'well-rounded' people talk to me about struggling to feel loved by God.

Do you believe you are loved by God? ____

What do you think you would have to do to get Him to love you more than He already does?

____

____

____

As you have read in this book and hopefully realized from all the questions you have answered, there is nothing we can do to get God to love us more than He already does.

As He continues to draw us close to Him and heals our broken places, He instills a supernatural love within us that is contagious. What He wants us to do with it is reach out and share it. Start with those closest to us, our family, friends and coworkers. Next we can move on to those at the coffee shop, gas station, gym and grocery store.

Who in your life needs God's love?

____

____

____

What about the people in your life that you can't stand? The people you actually believe got put here to make your life a living hell? Why on earth would God have these horrific people in your life?

Do you have anyone in your life that you utterly despise?

____

____

____

Why do you despise them?

____

____

____

For whatever reason, God thought it would be a good idea for them to be in your life. Would you be willing to pray for them for a solid two weeks? Ask God to do whatever He needs to do in their lives so they can be healed and whole.

The one thing prayer will do is set you free from the uncomfortable feelings you experience from being in their presence or thinking about them. God surely doesn't want us bound up with forgiveness and discord.

I have plenty of stories where people were very mean to me through the years. As I have prayed for them, God has brought me peace and has given me the strength to be cordial to them.

We never know what is going on in other's worlds to make them the way they are. Perhaps it is your prayers that will help them start their path to freedom!

Are you willing to take that chance? ____________________________________

Imagine how incredible you will feel if God truly started using you to help heal this broken and unraveling generation in which we find ourselves. What if no one ever prayed for us? Where would we be? What if everyone held all the ugliness within us against us? Please take this time to talk to God about any ugliness you have stored up in your heart. He wants to love you deeply as He sets you free so you can be His light in what can sometimes be a very dark world!

It's your turn:

Rise Up

So another new year was upon us. It was an election year and everyone believed this was going to be the best year ever...after all it was 2020. What kind of amazing things can people accomplish this year?

What goals did you have for yourself as you entered 2020?

I had been contracting with Children's Protective Services and had become busier than I wanted to be. At one point, I truly felt like I was drowning from all the clients and didn't know how to catch my breath. It was then that I felt like God encouraged me to make an appointment with Him. It wasn't that I didn't spend time with Him, but I was certainly not being changed as a result.

My goal was to work hard and get my stupid credit card paid in full. I was willing to do whatever I had to do to make that happen! I had a plan and I wasn't going to let anything stop me! Nothing, that is, except the pandemic that shut down not only the USA but the whole world!

COVID 19 hit and everything went crazy. People were panicking everywhere. All the sporting events, spring breaks, church events, literally everything came to a screeching halt. Then there were the riots that destroyed many major cities, as well as wild fires and hurricanes. The unrest in America was apparent to all.

After a few months, life started slowly coming back together again. Not only did God help me get the credit card paid but He also encouraged me to get ready for the next leg of our journey together. He started showing me that my mission was to make people's lives a better place to be.

As I pondered the few years prior, I realized how obsessed I was with being the executive director of Alive at Last Ministries. I was so upset because I didn't believe I was qualified for the position, I was afraid I wouldn't know how to act, that wealthy people might try to outsmart or control me. My internal world obviously needed an overhaul.

After some thorough cleansing and a whole lot of emotional healing, I realize I don't have to be concerned about any of those things. I am very clear I am anything but perfect; I humbly have to be who I was created to be. Jesus has my heart and my back so my job is to simply follow His leading in all I do and apologize should a mistake be made.

With that said, I had an invite to attend a prayer group. Not knowing what I was getting myself into, I agreed to give it a try. When I arrived for the group, there was only the host. Everyone else couldn't make it that day. It was then that the host told me she accidently sent me the request so it was obvious God wanted me there. We both laughed.

The second week, another gal joined us. During that group she spoke over me and told me it was time to 'RISE UP!' Wondering what that would look like, I went home to ponder it. The whole next day, those words kept coming to me.

When I went back for the next session, more ladies were there and one of them said to me that she could see I was a mighty warrior going in to help my clients get free from their bondages. Well, I was surprised to hear that because sometimes I don't feel like I am a mighty warrior, especially when asking God to search me and He show me what needs to be removed!

God radically blew me away with this group. I had tried to be in groups in the past few years but wasn't able to really connect. He then had my family move to another church in the city of my ministry. So now He put me in a group with ladies from the church we just left. Why did He wait until we left the church to give me that small group? Could it be He knew I would not want to leave the church if I had close knit connections with a cozy group?

The funny thing about my new group is they seem very confident in their own skin. They don't have pasts like mine. They are very put together and beautiful in their own way. Each of them have an incredible relationship with God and the way they are teaching me to pray is amazing.

Talk about groups you have attended and the outcome of them:

____

____

____

Were you able to make lasting connections? ____________________________

In the last several months, God has been teaching me how to be who He created me to be. He doesn't want me competing or comparing myself with anyone else. He designed me to be who He needed me to be to work with the population He called me to work with.

I have spent more time than I care to admit wishing I was like others. What a waste of time! God creates us to do the work He calls us to do. There are many people who I will never be able to resonate with and that is alright. There are enough people out there that I will connect with and who will want my help to keep me busy for the rest of my days.

Do you spend time wishing you were like someone else? ______________________

If so, who and why?

____

____

____

In case you hadn't noticed, our world is unraveling at record speed. God needs us to be who He created us to be so we can help those He has called us to help. I guarantee you, you will never be happier than when you are living your calling.

In a couple weeks, I am going to be 54 years old. I am not Mrs. Muscular anymore, nor is my skin taut and without cellulite, but I am getting more comfortable with who I was created to be. The more comfortable I become, the more able I will be to help people become who they were created to be. As they do the work necessary to become whole, the happier they will become and the less addicted they will be to all the meaningless things that keep them distracted and stuck in the misery of an adventure-less life.

Are you ready to be all in for what God has for you? ______________________________

What are the areas of your life that stand in the way of you following Him wholeheartedly?

____

____

____

What do you think He is calling you to do?

____

____

____

Do you trust Him enough to give Him your all and see what happens? __________________

I promise you will not be disappointed if you surrender your life to Him. I have certainly endured hard times but they are nothing compared to the messes I constantly found myself in when I let my will run riot! He has an amazing plan for you, He is just waiting for you to grab His Hand so the two of you can get started.

Then I heard the Lord asking, "Whom should I send as a messenger to this people?
Who will go for us?" I said,

"Here I am. Send Me!"

Isaiah 6:8 NLT

It's your turn:

Dear Lord Jesus,

I may not know what I am getting myself into here,
but I am willing to give you a shot.
As best as I am able, I surrender myself to you.
You know probably far better than I all the broken and bruised places within me.
Places that have been walled off for years that I have never wanted to see again.
Places I thought would go with me to the grave.
Lord, if those places are rendering me ineffective, I pray you tenderly do
what you need to do with them so I can be healed and whole.
I don't want to finish this race addicted to the many things I think I need to make me happy.
I want to try to give you a chance to make me happy.
Here I am, do with me as you will to create me into the person you designed me to be.
If I try to run because the process gets painful,
please put people in my life to guide me back to you.
And on that note, if there are people in my life that will lead me away from you,
please remove them...and help me see it is for my own wellbeing.
God, I want to learn about your love.
I want to be who you made me to be without all the extra baggage I now carry.

Jesus, I have made many mistakes through the years. I have had a lot of guilt and shame.
Please take all of it and do whatever you want with it.
I want to be healed and whole.
I want to be everything you have created me to be.
As I embark on this journey, please guide my steps.
I don't want to be held captive any longer in this place called life.
Jesus, I want to be free. Please show me what I need to do so I can have that.
In Jesus Name I Pray, Amen!

For I know the plans I have for you," declares the LORD,
"plans to prosper you and not to harm you, plans to give you hope and a future.
Then you will call on me and come and pray to me, and I will listen to you.
You will seek me and find me when you seek me with all your heart. I will be found by you,"
declares the LORD, "and will bring you back from captivity...."
Jer 29:11-14a NIV

The Year of the LORD'S Favor

Final Assessment

Isaiah 61:1-4

The Spirit of the Sovereign LORD is upon me

What would it look like to have the Spirit of the Sovereign LORD be upon you?

____

____

____

Because the LORD has anointed me

What would it look like to be anointed and would you want that?

____

____

____

To proclaim good news to the poor.

In what ways do you feel poor?

____

____

____

He has sent me to bind up the brokenhearted,

What has broken your heart?

____

____

____

To proclaim freedom for the captives

In what ways do you feel like a captive?

____

____

____

And release from darkness for the prisoners.

What is your darkness? What makes you feel like a prisoner?

____

____

____

To proclaim the year of the LORD's favor
What would the LORD'S favor look like in your life?

And the day of vengeance of our God
Where do you want to see God's vengeance?

To comfort all who mourn
Where do you need to be comforted?

And provide for those who grieve in Zion
What is causing you to grieve?

To bestow on them a crown of beauty
How would your life be different if you had a crown of beauty?

Instead of ashes
What ashes do you need to surrender to Jesus?

The oil of joy

What would your life look like with the 'oil of joy'?

Instead of mourning,

What is causing you to mourn?

And a garment of praise

What would your life look like if you wrapped it in praise?

Instead of a spirit of despair.

What has caused you to have a spirit of despair?

They will be called oaks of righteousness,

What would your life look like being an oak of righteousness?

A planting of the LORD for the display of His splendor.

Imagine being planted by the LORD to be a display of His splendor.

They will rebuild the ancient ruins
What ruins need to be rebuilt in your life?

____

____

____

And restore the places long devastated;
What has been long devastated in your life?

____

____

____

They will renew the ruined cities
What would your ruined city look like if it was renewed?

____

____

____

That have been devastated for generations.
What in your life has been devastated for generations?

____

____

____

If you would like to contact Suzanna directly, please send email inquiries to: suzannawarren@gmail.com

Made in USA - Kendallville, IN
1195417_9781726736077
11.17.2020 0947